RICHLAND HILLS &

INSTRUMENTAL MUSIC

A Plea to Reconsider

Dave Miller, Ph.D.

Apologetics Press, Inc.
230 Landmark Dr.
Montgomery, AL 36117-2752

Sain Publications
P.O. Box 616
Pulaski, TN 38478

© Copyright 2007
ISBN 10: 1-60063-30-49
ISBN 13: 978-1-60063-004-0

Cover by Rob Baker
Text set by Jim Estabrook

Library of Congress Cataloging-in-Publication

Dave Miller (1953 -)

Richland Hills & Instrumental Music: A Plea to Reconsider

Includes bibliographic references.

ISBN 10: 1-60063-30-49   ISBN 13: 978-1-60063-004-0

1. Public worship & other practices. 2. Christianity & Christian theology. 3. Sacraments, other rites & acts. I. Title.

203-dc22   2007903519

DEDICATION
To Deb—
whose positive influence on my life
has been inestimable, profound,
and eternal.

TABLE OF CONTENTS

Charts

Preface

The church that claims to be the largest church of Christ in America now conducts a 5:00 p.m. Saturday afternoon worship service that incorporates both the Lord's Supper and instrumental music (Ross, 2007). In preparation for this historically significant departure from past practice, Rick Atchley delivered three sermons (all titled "The Both/And Church") in December 2006 from the Richland Hills pulpit in an effort to explain the rationale behind the change (2006). This book constitutes a critical review of the contentions contained in those sermons that purport to justify the use of instrumental music in Christian worship. The reader is encouraged to secure Rick's sermons and give them a fair and equal hearing in conjunction with the critique that follows (see Atchley, 2006). [NOTE: Due to Rick's reliance on the NIV, that version is used repeatedly in this critique.]

No human on Earth today has the power to look into the heart of his fellowman and ascertain the man's true motives. We are called upon by God to think the best, believe the best, and hope the best about each other (1 Corinthians 13:7). I absolutely refuse to question Rick's motives, or charge him with deliberate misrepresentation of the facts. I desire to attribute to him the same sincerity that I would like him to ascribe to me. I have no desire to "nit pick" Rick's sermons. My sole desire is to ascertain God's truth on matters that will affect our eternal destiny. This is serious business. And the matter of how to worship God has eternal consequences—souls are at stake.

Since God admonishes every accountable person to be a sincere seeker of truth (Proverbs 23:23; John 7:17), genuine Christians should have no hesitation in examining contrary viewpoints. My prayer is that those who have accepted the claims and conclusions that Rick has offered will be willing to give the contrary viewpoint an honest hearing. With humility I offer the following critique of Rick's claims.

Richland Hills and Instrumental Music: A Plea to Reconsider

Dave Miller, Ph.D.

*"The first one to plead his cause seems right, until
his neighbor comes and examines him."*

Proverbs 18:17

Jesus insisted that we are to examine fruit (Matthew 7:15-20), put everything to the test (1 Thessalonians 5:21), and not believe every spirit, but test them (1 John 4:1). While I do not question my brother's motives or sincerity, I am puzzled and deeply disturbed about his failure to divulge all relevant evidence to his hearers—especially since he claims personally to have engaged in a fair consideration of both sides of the issue: "I spent **three days** in Abilene in the library, reading everything I could read on this subject. I let every side have their best shot at me. I read debates that were 100 years old. **I read everything the anti-instrument position has produced**." Really? I can only assume that Rick made a slip of the tongue or spoke hyperbolically. After all, that would mean he read—

The 1903 *Stark-Warlick Debate*—198 pages

The 1908 *Otey-Briney Debate*—299 pages

The 1921 *Colley-Tyndall Debate*—31 pages

The 1923 *Boswell-Hardeman Debate*—239 pages

The 1927 *Clubb-Boles Debate*—155 pages

The 1942 *Hunt-Inman Debate*—178 pages

The 1950 *Wallace-Barber Debate*—275 pages

The 1976 *Shelly-Dunning Debate*—198 pages

The 1988 *Highers-Blakely Debate*—279 pages

John T. Lewis, *Voice of the Pioneers on Instrumental Music*—291 pgs

M.C. Kurfees, *Instrumental Music in the Worship*—278 pages

E.C. Fuqua, *Instrumental Music in Worship is Sinful*

James Bales, *Instrumental Music and N.T. Worship*—299 pages

Foy Wallace, *The Instrumental Music Question*—344 pages

J.E. Choate/W. Woodson, *Sounding Brass & Clanging Cymbals*

Rubel Shelly, *Sing His Praise!: A Case for A Cappella Music*

E. Ferguson, J. Lewis, E. West, *The I. Music Issue*—102 pages

FHU 1991 Forum: *Instrumental Music: Faith or Opinion?*—186 pgs

Numbering well over 3,000 pages, these sources represent only a small fraction of the materials produced within churches of Christ just in the last 100 years, not to mention the host of tracts, journal articles, booklets, and sermons on the subject. That's a lot of reading for three days.

In any case, the fact of the matter is that Rick poses no new thoughts in his advocacy of instrumental music. All his points were thoroughly examined and decisively defeated long ago. Those who fail to acquaint themselves with past mistakes are doomed to repeat them.

"THE BOTH/AND CHURCH—PART I"

The first sermon that Rick preached (December 3, 2006) was prefatory in nature and did not claim to offer any scriptural proof for the introduction of instrumental music into the worship assembly. However, Rick made several assertions that create the impression that those who are **for** the instrument are more interested in positive "progress," more "faithful to God's Word and Christ's mission," and are less guilty of "making it harder for a sinner to come to Christ" than those who **oppose** the instrument. Yet, all these allegations beg the question and only prejudice the hearer. It is not uncommon for the progressive to label those who resist his illicit change as resistant to "progress." Yet the progress to which Rick refers rightfully fits under the category of the Greek term used in 2 John 9, *proago*, translated variously "transgresses" (NKJV), "runs ahead" (NIV), and "goes too far" (NASB).

Certainly no genuine Christian desires to "make it harder for a sinner to come to Christ," but neither should the genuine Christian desire to **make it easier than Christ Himself made it**. Is Jesus guilty of making it harder for sinners to come to Him by requiring immersion (John 3:5)? The only issue to be settled is whether God permits or prohibits instrumental music in worship.

Yet, consider: what honest, sincere person, having heard the pure Gospel, having learned what God has done for us in Christ and the rich spiritual blessings that accompany that sacrifice, would balk at complete submission to Christ simply on the grounds that the worship of God excludes a humanly-devised, mechanical contraption? Answer: only one who has not had a genuine change of mind (repentance), and who is reluctant to render complete allegiance to Christ to the point of abandoning **fleshly allurements**! How far will Rick go to accommodate the worldly desires of potential church members? Since large numbers of people are enamored with sprinkling babies with water, will Rick bring this practice into the church, lest he be guilty of making it harder for people to come to Christ? Billions have failed to come to the conclusion that Jesus Christ is God—will Rick compromise this doctrine as well in order to make it easier for people to come to Christ?

The same may be said of Rick's passionate, but revealing, assertion: "I know this, if our fellowship [a sectarian expression in itself—DM] stays on the course we're currently on, the future looks bleak. Someone has got to be a leader." Really? The future of the church depends, **not** on the worldwide preaching of the Gospel, **not** on the faithful, pure living of that Gospel by Christians, and **not** on the fervent prayers of the saints. Oh, no. **The very future of the church depends on *the introduction of the instrument into worship*!** With all the kindness and goodwill I can muster, I insist that such a statement is preposterous, ludicrous, and unbiblical. It betrays an immature, unspiritual, fleshly appraisal of biblical reality. What's more, Rick and Richland Hills deem **themselves** to be the leaders to save the church and to get the rest of us on track? Perhaps a good dose of Proverbs 16:18 and 18:12 would be in order.

May I kindly suggest that Rick has misconstrued the concept of "legalism" by labeling those who oppose instrumental music as legalists—when, in fact, they are merely wanting to make certain that they are **legal in God's eyes**, i.e., obedient to His will. On the other hand, those who introduce instrumental music are **illegalists**, thereby placing themselves in the unenviable position of disrespecting God's law and flouting His desire that we **be loving by being legal** (John 14:15; Romans 13:8-10; Ecclesiastes 12:13).

"THE BOTH/AND CHURCH—PART 2"

In the second sermon (December 10, 2006), Rick proceeds to set forth alleged **biblical** justification for introducing the instrument into the worship assembly. He prefaced these points with some rather condescending, ungracious assessments of those who have refrained from using instruments in worship. For one, he insisted that those who oppose the instrument have been guilty for years of dividing the body of Christ. Such an accusation is outrageous. Historical fact: Those who **introduced** the instrument are the ones who disrupted the unity of the body. As Joe Warlick rightly noted in 1903 in Henderson, Tennessee: "Every one knows that those who have introduced and brought in the divisive things, including instrumental music, into the worship of the saints are alone and altogether responsible for the division" (Stark and Warlick, p. 20; cf. 1 Kings 18:17; Luke 12:51; 1 Corinthians 11:19).

Rick then explained, "I'm going to share with you now in this session a lesson that I knew years ago I was gonna have to

4

teach if I was gonna have any integrity at all." Pointing behind himself on the stage, Rick announced:

> Right there at that spot about 1994 **the Holy Spirit said to me in the middle of my sermon**, "and that's what you and all the preachers like you were doing, who haven't for years believed that the worship of God with instruments is wrong. But you continue by your silence to let people think it's wrong, to allow the body to be disrupted, and you do so under the plea, 'Well, we're just maintaining peace.' But that's not peace; that's cowardice." I knew then the day would come I'd have to teach this lesson (emp. added).

If the Holy Spirit rebuked Rick for neglecting to speak forth regarding the acceptability of instruments, why did he not obey the Holy Spirit **immediately**? Why did he wait **12 years** to obey Him? Why did he wait **12 years** to, in his words, "have any integrity at all"? Rick had **a direct word from God** that remaining silent on instruments was allowing the body of Christ to be disrupted, yet **he spurned acting in harmony with that divine prodding for over a decade!** So from at least 1994 to 2006, by his own admission, Rick had little or no integrity. Never mind the fact that the Holy Spirit does not speak directly to people today (see Miller, 2003a, 23[3]:17-23).

Further, Rick insisted:

> The truth is, almost no one reading the Bible sincerely for the first time would ever conclude that instrumental praise is unacceptable to God. That statement is so strong I need to say it again. I contend you give this Bible to any sincere person with no preconceived conditions and say, "Just read it and find out what God wants of you," that no one, just reading this Bible, would conclude that instrumental praise is unacceptable to God.

Not only is such a claim intolerant, judgmental, arrogant, divisive, and unkind, it is untrue. The fact is that millions of Christians—including the first-century Christians—came to

5

the very conclusion that Rick rejects. His statement implies that the millions of members of churches of Christ who have rejected the use of the instrument through the centuries have all been insincere, biased, and fraught with "preconceived conditions"; they have lacked the integrity to buck the status quo. Rick's insult applies equally to the millions of Greek Orthodox Church members, dating back to the eleventh century, as well as to those who orchestrated the Reformation Movement in the 16th and 17th centuries, from Zwingli to Calvin, who condemned the use of instrumental music in worship. For example, John Calvin declared:

> A difference is to be observed in this respect between his people under the Old and under the New Testament; for now that Christ is appeared, and the Church has reached full age, it were only to bury the light of the Gospel, should we introduce the shadows of a departed dispensation. From this, it appears that the Papists, in employing **instrumental music**, cannot be said so much to imitate the practice of God's ancient people, as to **ape it in a senseless and absurd manner**, exhibiting a **silly delight** in that worship of the Old Testament which was figurative, and **terminated with the Gospel** (1999, 3:495, emp. added; cf. 3:98,312; 5:312).

(For a summary of the views of the Reformers regarding instrumental music, see 19th century Columbia Theological Seminary Presbyterian professor Dr. John Girardeau, 1888, pp. 90ff.).

In contrast, Rick insists that those who choose to use the instrument have an equally high regard for the Bible as those who reject its use. That may well be true, but the assertion is irrelevant and beside the point. Saul also claimed high regard for God's Word (1 Samuel 15:13,20-21). The fact that one billion people on Earth **sincerely believe** that a mere man who sits in the Vatican in Rome is literally Christ's vicar on Earth with full authority to speak directly for Christ does not make it so. The fact that 1.3 billion people on Earth

passionately and sincerely believe that Muhammad was the final and greatest prophet of God does not make it so. Sincerity, conviction, and high regard for the Bible are no guarantee that the truth is being embraced (e.g., Acts 26:9). **Both** sincerity **and** truth are necessary to please God (Joshua 24:14; John 4:24; 1 Corinthians 5:8). Our love for God must surpass mere words or claims by being coupled with actions and truth (1 John 3:18). It's not enough to worship God with "reverence and awe"; we must worship Him "**acceptably**" (Hebrews 12:28)—because "our 'God is a consuming fire'" (vs. 29). *That's the true "Both/ And" church.*

"Old Testament Reasons for Accepting Instrumental Music"

Rick offers three Old Testament reasons for accepting instrumental music:

I/II. Commanded and Blessed

The first two reasons assert that under the Old Testament, God did not just allow instrumental music, He **commanded and blessed it**. Rick offered the following passages for these contentions: 2 Chronicles 5:13-14; 7:6; 29:25-26; Psalm 33:1-3; 92:1-3; 150:1-6. Response: Rick is absolutely correct in these assertions. It is true that some among the "anti-instrument" viewpoint (as Rick styles it) have claimed that God never approved, but only tolerated, the instrument in Old Testament worship. Rick ridiculed this viewpoint with the rhetorical question: "[I]s that standing **under** the word of God or **over** the word of God?" The fact is the **majority** of those within churches of Christ have long acknowledged the divinely approved use of instruments **in Old Testament Jewish worship**. But this realization is completely beside the point and side-steps the issue. Why?

1. One cannot assume that simply because God approved of a worship practice under Judaism, He likewise approves

of it in Christian worship. The Jews were under a completely different and distinct religious system than the one under which Christians serve (cf. Jeremiah 31:31-34; Hebrews 8:7-13). Christ and the Christian system were certainly foreshadowed in the Old Testament, being woven into the fabric of Scripture from the beginning. Types and shadows abound in the Old Testament (Colossians 2:17; Hebrews 8:5; 10:1). The various aspects of the Old Covenant were clearly designed and preordained to prefigure and foreshadow the New—they were "copies of the true" (Hebrews 9:24). Israelite life and worship conducted in 1500 B.C. was preplanned and divinely orchestrated to anticipate Christian living after A.D. 30. **However, one must examine each act of worship in order to determine whether an act or practice under the Mosaic system has any bearing on Christian worship.** How may one ascertain which aspects of Jewish worship are perpetuated in Christian worship? Obviously, one must go to the **New** Testament to see what Jesus and His emissaries said, and how first-century Christians then carried out those directives. Doing so forces one to the conclusion that Christians did not incorporate instrumental music into their musical worship in the first-century—though the first Christians were Jews.

2. To see the logical fallacy of Rick's reasoning on this point, ask yourself whether all the **other** acts of worship under the Old Testament are to be practiced today as well. What about dancing (Psalm 150:4)? Sadly, some are introducing "sacred dance" into their worship. What about burning incense (Exodus 25:6)? Some may say, yes, we can burn incense, too—and candles. But burning candles is not burning incense; and where in the Bible did God ever desire the burning of candles in worship? [NOTE: the golden lampstand of the Jewish tabernacle did not utilize candles, but rather oil lamps. "Candle" is a mistranslation and occurs nowhere in the original languages of the Bible.]

Is Rick prepared to return to the Old Testament worship rituals connected to the Jewish temple, the Ark, and the Sabbath? After all, God **commanded and blessed** these, too (e.g., Exodus 20:8-11). Likewise, the Old Testament firmly asserts that **God was pleased** with animal sacrifices and other offerings: "Then You shall be **pleased** with the sacrifices of righteousness, **with burnt offering and whole burnt offering**; then they shall offer bulls on Your altar" (Psalm 51:19, emp. added). Six times in Numbers 15, the animal, grain, and liquid offerings brought by the Israelites are described as "an **aroma pleasing to the Lord.**" In fact, at the very time that Jesus and John arrived on the scene to launch Christianity, John's father offered incense, as reported by Luke: "Once when Zechariah's division was on duty and he was serving as priest before God, he was chosen by lot, according to the custom of the priesthood, to go into the temple of the Lord **and burn incense.** And **when the time for the burning of incense came, all the assembled worshipers were praying outside**" (Luke 1:8-10, NIV, emp. added). Will Richland Hills "lead the way" in mimicking these practices as well? They had better be very careful doing so, since God issued a warning to the Jews on the matter:

> Then the LORD said to Moses, "Take fragrant spices—gum resin, onycha and galbanum—and pure frankincense, all in equal amounts, and make a fragrant blend of incense, the work of a perfumer. It is to be salted and pure and sacred. Grind some of it to powder and place it in front of the Testimony in the Tent of Meeting, where I will meet with you. It shall be most holy to you. **Do not make any incense with this formula for yourselves;** consider it holy to the LORD. **Whoever makes any like it to enjoy its fragrance must be cut off from his people**" (Exodus 30:34-38, NIV, emp. added).

God also required the Jews to create a sacred anointing oil to be used to anoint the worship facility, utensils and accessories, as well as the priests (Exodus 30:22-32). Since all Christians are priests (1 Peter 2:5,9; Revelation 1:6), will Rick and Richland Hills begin anointing the pews, the communion table/trays, the pulpit, and each other in their worship assembly? Careful, this practice, too, came with a stern warning (Exodus 30:33).

Rick insisted: "There is not a hint anywhere in the Bible that God was ever anything but pleased by instrumental praise offered from a sincere heart." To see the error of this argument, simply insert into his statement in place of "instrumental praise" any of the above Old Testament actions. For example: "There is not a hint anywhere in the Bible that God was ever anything but pleased by **observing the Sabbath** from a sincere heart." "There is not a hint anywhere in the Bible that God was ever anything but pleased by **cereal offerings** from a sincere heart." "There is not a hint anywhere in the Bible that God was ever anything but pleased by **observing the Passover** from a sincere heart." It will do no good to claim that these activities were replaced or surpassed under the New Covenant. The same may be claimed for instrumental music—it is obsolete and surpassed by pure *a cappella* singing. Rick's argument is that since God **commanded and was pleased** with instrumental music under the Old Testament, He must necessarily be pleased with it under the New. But that contention is false.

The fact of the matter is that dancing, the burning of incense, the offering of sacrifices, Sabbath observance, use of anointing oil, wine, cereal, and, yes, the use of instruments, are all outdated, inferior, "weak and useless" (Hebrews 7:18), "obsolete" (Hebrews 8:13) practices that manifest disrespect for the "new order," the "new and living way," and the "better things" of Christ's religion (cf. Hebrews 9:10; 6:9; 10:20). While the Old Testament foreshadowed the New, it cannot provide direction for worship under the New. The Old Testament says nothing concerning the Lord's Supper. We must go to the New to learn God's will on that matter. While Mosaic Law included praying and singing, their inclusion in Christian worship must be determined on the basis of their treatment in the New. In fact, both are forthrightly enjoined in the New Testament—**instruments are not**.

How are we to determine how to worship God under the New Covenant? Rather than going to the Old Testament and selectively picking and choosing what will be brought over into Christian worship, the biblical, logical approach is to go to the New Testament and find out what God enjoins there. Rick scolded the "anti-instrumentalist" for wanting to confine worship protocol to the New; yet he desires to return to the Old—without using **all** the Old. Which approach is more consistent—let alone biblical? Which approach is standing **over** the Word of God, and which is standing **under** the Word of God?

Rick noted: "By the way, remember that God declared a musician to be a man after His own heart." Does that prove that God wants instruments of music used in **Christian** worship? No. Does that mean that Christians who are **not** musicians are not after God's own heart? No. Was David said to be after God's own heart **because** he was a musician? Of course not. David was also a shepherd. Does that prove that we ought to herd sheep in worship?

3. Rick stated: "Now remember, these are the very psalms we are commanded in the New Testament to read and to sing. Now doesn't it seem odd to you the Holy Spirit would command us to sing psalms we are forbidden to practice?" But wait. Let us follow his logic: Since we are commanded to read/sing psalms in the New Testament, it follows that we are permitted to practice whatever is sanctioned in those psalms. That would include animal sacrifice:

➤ "Make a joyful shout to God, all the earth! Sing out the honor of His name; Make His praise glorious....
I will offer You burnt sacrifices of fat animals,

11

with the sweet aroma of rams; I will offer bulls with goats" (Psalm 66:1-2,15, emp. added).

What about facing Jerusalem while worshipping?

> "I will praise You with my whole heart; before the gods I will sing praises to You. **I will worship toward Your holy temple**, and praise Your name" (Psalm 138:1-2, emp. added).

What about worshipping God from His holy hill, i.e., in Jerusalem at the tabernacle and Jewish altar?

> "Oh, send out Your light and Your truth! Let them lead me; Let them bring me to **Your holy hill and to Your tabernacle**. Then I will go to **the altar of God**, to God my exceeding joy; and on the harp I will praise You, O God, my God (Psalm 43:3-4, emp. added).

> "Exalt the LORD our God, and **worship at His holy hill**; For the LORD our God is holy" (Psalm 99:9, emp. added).

Indeed, one of the very psalms that Rick uses to sanction instrumental music says, "Praise God **in His sanctuary**" (Psalm 150:1)—which does not refer to a church building in Fort Worth, Texas.

What about dashing babies' heads against rocks?

> "There on the poplars we hung **our harps**.... How shall we sing the LORD's song in a foreign land? ...O daughter of Babylon, who are to be destroyed, happy the one who repays you as you have served us! **Happy the one who takes and dashes your little ones against the rock!**" (Psalm 137:2,4,8-9, emp. added).

What about moving beds and swords into the assembly?

> "Let the saints rejoice in this honor and sing for joy **on their beds**" with "a **double-edged sword in their hands**" (Psalm 149:5-6).

Three additional points that Rick overlooked: (1) Though New Testament writers alluded to many of the Old Testament psalms, **none include any of the references to instruments**. If Rick's claim that the use of instrumental music in the Psalms was intended to serve as a precedent for Christians, you would think at least one reference to instrumental music from the Psalms would be mentioned in the New Testament; (2) The instruments listed in Psalm 33 and 150 were not optional—they were **commanded**. It is not enough for Richland Hills merely to include just any instrument. Rick noted: "By the way, did you know there are over 20 kinds of musical instruments mentioned in the Old Testament with which you can praise God?" So to obey the **command** of God, they **must** use the harp, the psaltery, the instrument of 10 strings, the trumpet, timbrel, organ, cymbals, etc.; (3) the use of instruments under the Old Law was confined to **the male priests and Levites**—"the privilege of belonging to which was based upon natural descent.... They formed **a separate and exclusive order**, to which none were admitted but **those descended from a particular family**" (Schurer, 1890, 1:225,271; cf. 1:226,269-273,290). This fact is stated explicitly in the very passages Rick used:

> **The priests** then withdrew from the Holy Place. All **the priests** who were there had consecrated themselves, regardless of their divisions. All **the Levites who were musicians**—Asaph, Heman, Jeduthun and their sons and relatives—stood on the east side of the altar, dressed in fine linen and playing cymbals, harps and lyres. They were accompanied by 120 **priests** sounding trumpets (2 Chronicles 5:11-12).
>
> **The priests** took their positions, as did **the Levites** with the LORD's musical instruments, which King David had made for praising the LORD and which were used when he gave thanks, saying, "His love endures forever." Opposite **the Levites, the priests** blew their trumpets, and all the Israelites were standing (2 Chronicles 7:6).
>
> He stationed **the Levites** in the temple of the LORD with cymbals, harps and lyres in the way prescribed by David

and Gad the king's seer and Nathan the prophet; this was commanded by the LORD through his prophets. So **the Levites** stood ready with David's instruments, and **the priests** with their trumpets (2 Chronicles 29:25-26, emp. added).

Rick says nothing about the fact that the rank and file Jewish worshippers, including all the women, did not play instruments and would have been disobedient if they had presumed to do so (cf. Numbers 16:8-10,40). On what principle of exegesis is this restriction to be ignored today? If all Christians are priests (1 Peter 2:5,9; Revelation 1:6; 5:10), then all must play an instrument in worship.

4. Rick insists that "God commanded instrumental praise **before** the law was given." He bases the assertion on the actions of Miriam and the other women after crossing the Red Sea (Exodus 15:20), as well as on Psalm 81:1-5. But the use of instrumental music in worship under the Christian era cannot be decided on the basis of what the Gentiles did under Patriarchy anymore than what the Jews did under the Law of Moses. We are to refrain from lying today, not because lying was sinful during the Patriarchal or Mosaic periods, but because it is sinful under the Law of Christ (Ephesians 4:25). We cannot justify the use of instruments on the grounds that Adam, Noah, Abraham, Moses, Miriam, or David used them. We must base our practices solely on the will of Christ under the New Covenant (cf. John 12:48; Hebrews 9:15-17). As Methodist commentator Adam Clarke noted in his remarks on Psalm 81: "He must be ill off for proofs in favour of instrumental music in the Church of Christ, who has recourse to practices under the Jewish ritual" (n.d., 3:477).

Observe carefully the misuse and misapplication of Psalm 81:1-5—

Sing aloud to God our strength; Make a joyful shout to the God of Jacob.

Raise a song and strike the timbrel, the pleasant harp with the lute.

Blow the trumpet at the time of the New Moon, at the full moon, on our solemn feast day.

For this is a statute **for Israel**, a law of the God **of Jacob**.

This He established **in Joseph** as a testimony, **when He went throughout the land of Egypt**,

Where I heard a language I did not understand (emp. added).

Three clarifications demonstrate Rick's misapplication of the passage:

(1) This psalm is directed to the Levites, as indicated by the preliminary notation, "For the director of music. According to *gittith*. Of Asaph," explained in the following passage:

> He [David—DM] appointed some of the Levites to minister before the ark of the LORD, to make petition, to give thanks, and to praise the LORD, the God of Israel: **Asaph was the chief**, Zechariah second, then Jeiel, Shemiramoth, Jehiel, Mattithiah, Eliab, Benaiah, Obed-Edom and Jeiel. They were to play the lyres and harps, Asaph was to sound the cymbals, and Benaiah and Jahaziel the priests were to blow the trumpets regularly before the ark of the covenant of God (1 Chronicles 16:4-6; cf. 1 Chronicles 25; 2 Chronicles 30:21).

So Psalm 81 pertains to the actions of the Levites, with Asaph as chief, and provides no assistance in ascertaining how Christians are to worship.

(2) The blowing of the trumpet at the New Moon had nothing to do with instrumental praise. Rather, a single trumpet blast was to be sounded (only by the priests) to alert the entire community of the commencement of the prescribed rituals associated with the Jewish festivals (Numbers 10:10). The silver trumpets were also used to sound assembly, to coordinate tribal travel sequence, and

to signal military engagement (Numbers 10:1-9). [NOTE: For discussions by Hebrew scholars on these technical matters pertaining to Israelite activities, see Leupold, 1959, pp. 585ff.; Keil and Delitsch, 1976b, 5:390ff.; Barnes, 1847a, 2:320ff.]

(3) It is true that both Exodus 15 and Psalm 81 allude to events that predate shortly the formal giving of the Law of Moses at Sinai. However, in both instances, **Israelites**—not the **Gentiles**—were the focus, and their post-bondage religious practices were simply precursors to the formalization that would soon transpire at Sinai. In fact, Psalm 81 is simply referring back to the enactment of the Passover as it was prescribed before the Law was formally imparted (Exodus 13). Gentiles were not commanded to keep the Passover. Hence, Miriam's actions in Exodus 15 and Psalm 81 provide no indication of the use of instruments **outside** the Jewish nation. [NOTE: If Miriam's actions are to be construed as relevant to anything today, they would apply to holding victory parades, since women in Israel had the custom of conducting a victory celebration after enemy engagements (cf. 1 Samuel 18:6ff.). They certainly provide no assistance in determining how to conduct Christian worship.]

A fitting summary of the fallacy of relying on the Psalms as justification for instrumental music in worship is seen in the remarks of the peerless scholar J.W. McGarvey written in the *Christian Standard* on November 30, 1895:

If any man who is a preacher believes that the apostle teaches the use of instrumental music in the church by enjoining the singing of psalms, he is one of those smatterers in Greek who can believe anything that he wishes to believe. When the wish is father of the thought, correct exegesis is like water on a duck's back (1910, p. 116).

III. Prophesied for the Kingdom?

The third reason offered from the Old Testament for using instruments is that "Messianic prophecy anticipated instrumental music would continue in the coming kingdom." Psalm 45:6-7 is the proof text for this claim. Rick maintained that the Spirit guided the Hebrews writer (in 1:8-9) to apply that psalm to Christ. He then makes an unwarranted leap that since the very next verse in Psalm 45, i.e., verse 8, makes an allusion to "the music of the strings," Christ must surely be pleased with instrumental music in worship. May I kindly suggest that such an assumption is not **EX**egesis, it is **EIS**egesis—and hermeneutical ventriloquism.

1. The Holy Spirit did not guide the Hebrews writer to include the reference to the stringed instruments in verse 8 with the two verses that foreshadowed Christ. As noted earlier, though allusions to instrumental music in worship occur, in Rick's words, "all through the Psalms," using his reasoning, one would surely expect to find at least one such allusion to instruments from the Psalms in the New Testament. Yet observe that **the Holy Spirit nowhere included any of these references in the New Testament**—an omission that is thunderous in its import! Simply because a particular passage from the Old Testament is quoted in the New does not mean that everything in that context was intended to apply to the New. This hermeneutical principle even applies to Messianic prophecies. For example, though 2 Samuel 7:12-13 refers to Christ, the reference to committing iniquity or doing wrong in verse 14 obviously does **not** apply to Christ—but to Solomon (cf. Psalm 34:17-20 and John 19:36).

2. No contextual reason exists to assume that the reference to the stringed instruments refers to worship. By Rick's own admission, the metaphor pertains to **a wedding**. Instruments were used in weddings, **not for worship** but as part of the

normal celebration that characterizes such festivities, even as they are used in secular culture today as the bride and groom enter the auditorium.

3. Even if the **entire** psalm is intended to be a metaphorical foreshadowing of Christ, to see that Rick's leap is contextually unwarranted, observe several other features in the psalm that unquestionably cannot be applied either literally or to Christian worship:

> ➤ "Gird your **sword** upon your side" (vs. 3)
>
> ➤ "In your majesty **ride forth** victoriously" (vs. 4)
>
> ➤ "Let your **sharp arrows** pierce the hearts of the king's enemies" (vs. 5)
>
> ➤ "All your **robes** are fragrant with **myrrh and aloes and cassia** (vs. 8)
>
> ➤ "from **palaces adorned with ivory**" (vs. 8)
>
> ➤ "at your right hand is **the royal bride in gold of Ophir**" (vs. 9)

A simple reading of the entire psalm easily demonstrates that it is filled with poetic imagery and that the details are metaphorical. In being applied typologically to Christ, **none** of the details are intended to be taken literally. Otherwise, in addition to using instrumental music, Richland Hills ought also to include swords, horses, arrows, richly perfumed robes, ivory palaces, and women clothed in gold from Ophir. In fact, if we are going to play this free and easy with the text, the fact that the bride's "virgin companions follow her" (vs. 14) would lend credibility to the Quran's claims (cf. *Surah* 2:25; 3:15; 56:36). [NOTE: Rick fails to mention the fact that scholars differ on the translation of Psalm 45:8 as it relates to instruments. The Hebrew could very well be translated to omit the reference to stringed instruments, as in the NKJV: "All Your garments are scented with myrrh and aloes and cassia, out of the ivory palaces, by which they have made You glad." The difference in Hebrew is whether a term is taken as a contraction or whether it is to be construed as the poetical form of a preposition (see *Biblia Hebraica Stuttgartensia*, 1966/77, p. 1128 note 9c; cf. Alexander, 1873, p. 204).] Rick further overlooked the fact that the Septuagint translation (which, ironically, he insists was the Bible of the first-century church) rendered the verse **with no allusion to instruments**: "Myrrh, and stacte, and cassia *are exhaled* from thy garments, and out of the ivory palaces, [vs. 9] with which kings' daughters have gladdened thee for thine honour..." (1970, p. 724, italics in orig.).

Instruments in *zamar*?

Appealing to Romans 15:8-9, Rick next argued that Paul quoted either Psalm 18:49 or Psalm 57:9, in which the Hebrew word *zamar* is used. His conclusion? **"You won't find a lexicon anywhere that fails to include instruments in defining what the word *zamar* meant."** In so stating, Rick leaves the impression that all occurrences in the Old Testament of the term *zamar* must, of necessity, refer to the playing of instrumental music. Unfortunately, Rick has completely misconstrued the lexical evidence. As M.C. Kurfees predicted in 1911:

> There is a right way, and there is a wrong way to use lexicons; and it is not strange that young minds, uninformed concerning the evolution of words in the history of a language, should be misled by, and hence misapply, a definition which they find in a lexicon.... This shows that, in unskillful hands, a lexicon may be so used as to appear to disprove what it really proves, and, vice versa, to prove what it really disproves. Hence, next to the value of a lexicon itself, is the importance of knowing how to use it (1911, p. 8, emp. added).

Here are the linguistic facts of the matter:

1. Psalm 18 is the psalm that David sang to God in the context of 2 Samuel 22, where it is recorded verbatim. The context of the psalm is David's thanksgiving to God because He "delivered him from the hand of all his enemies and from

the hand of Saul" (2 Samuel 22:1). Hence, contextually, the psalm merely reports what David said **he** would do in praising God under Judaism. **It certainly does not purport to be a description of what is done in the church** (cf. Lewis, 1987, p. 43). In fact, the context of Romans 15 has nothing to do with worship. Then why did Paul quote from the psalm? Paul alluded to the 2 Samuel narrative (and thus Psalm 18:49), along with three other Old Testament passages (Deuteronomy 32:43; Psalm 117:1; Isaiah 11:10), **to show the necessity of both Jew and Gentile accepting one another as fellow citizens in the kingdom.**

2. In his quotation of the psalm in Romans 15:9, Paul used the Greek term *exomologesomai* (as did the Septuagint), which has as its root meaning to confess, acknowledge, admit, declare openly (Danker, 2000, p. 351). Nothing in that word implies use of instruments. Yet, Paul placed that term in parallel construction to "sing praises" (where *psallo* is his rendering for the Hebrew *zamar*). Hence, both terms (i.e., *exomologesomai* and *psallo*) refer simply to **oral, verbal** expression to the exclusion of instrumental music. [NOTE: A discussion of *psallo* will follow.]

3. The Hebrew term found in Psalm 18:49 (*zamar*) had as its root meaning "to cut, prune" (Davidson, 1848, p. 239; Girdlestone, 1983, p. 242), as is clearly seen in Leviticus 25:3-4 and Isaiah 5:6. How do the Hebrew lexicons and concordances define this term?

Hebrew Lexicons

As a master of ancient Near Eastern languages, Benjamin Davidson gave the following analysis of *zamar* as conjugated in the Piel:

> (prop[erly] *to divide*, with reference to rhythmical numbers, hence) *to sing hymns, praises*, with ל [Hebrew prefix preposition meaning "to"] or the acc[usative] of the person celebrated,

20

with בְּ [Hebrew prefix preposition meaning "in" or "with"] of the instrument for accompaniment (1848, p. 239, italics and parentheses in orig., bracketed items added).

Observe that, according to this renowned lexicographer, the central meaning of *zamar* is **to sing hymns and praises**, and in order to understand that an instrument accompanies that singing, the object of *zamar* must have the Hebrew preposition (בְּ) prefixed to the object intended.

Hebrew lexicographer, William Gesenius, identified three meanings for *zamar* as they occur in the Piel: (1) "to sing"; (2) "to play on a musical instrument [or to sing so accompanied]"; (3) "to dance" (1847, p. 248, bracketed item in orig.). Observe carefully: the first meaning Gesenius gave for *zamar* is "to sing." Since he noted that *zamar* can also carry a second meaning—"to play on a musical instrument [or to sing so accompanied]," it is clear that his first meaning—"to sing"—refers to singing **without** instrumental accompaniment. Rick avoided mentioning this fact.

The Brown-Driver-Briggs *Hebrew and English Lexicon of the Old Testament* defines *zamar* in the Piel as "make music in praise of God...make music, melody," and then offers the following twofold breakdown: "1. of singing to (לְ) God" and "2. of playing musical instruments" (1906, p. 274).

Basing his analysis on the classic lexical work of Koehler-Baumgartner, William Holladay offers the following four meanings for *zamar*: (1) play an instrument, sing; (2) praise; (3) "absolutely sing, praise"; (4) "with *bᵉ* [Hebrew prefix preposition meaning "in" or "with"—DM] play an instrument" (1971, pp. 89-90). Again, observe that *zamar* can mean singing to the exclusion of a mechanical instrument, and when an instrument is intended, the instrument is named and preceded by the preposition.

In the *Theological Wordbook of the Old Testament*, Herbert Wolf defines *zamar* in the Piel as "sing, sing praise, make music"

(1980, 1:245). He, too, clarifies the fact that singing and playing are distinct concepts that may or may not be linked together in a single use of the term (e.g., "singing may not always be implied when *zamar* or its cognates occurs"). In other words, *zamar* can refer to (1) singing alone, (2) playing an instrument alone, or (3) singing while playing an instrument. This fact is underscored in the derivatives of *zamar,* which include the words "song, music" (*zimra*), "song" (*zamir*), "psalm" (*mizmor*), and "singer" (*zammar*).

Robert Girdlestone explains: "Another word largely used in the Psalms, and from which the Hebrew name for a psalm is derived, is **Zamar,** *to sing.* Originally it meant *to pluck,* or *prune* (as a vine). It came to signify *to play* (by plucking) a *musical instrument* or *to sing so accompanied*" (1983, p. 242, boldface and italics in orig.). Observe carefully that he defines *zamar* as "to sing." He then alludes to the progressive development of meaning by contrasting playing with singing. Even if the singing is accompanied by an instrument, the singing to which *zamar* refers is distinct from the playing, and an instrument is not inherent in the meaning of the word.

In the listing of the occurrences of *zamar* in the Piel in the Old Testament, George Wigram's classic Hebrew concordance identifies two listings for the Infinitive (i.e., Psalm 92:1; 147:1), 15 for the Imperative (i.e., 1 Chronicles 16:9; Psalm 9:11; 30:4; 33:2; 47:6 [four times],7; 66:2; 68:4,32; 98:4,5; 105:2; 135:3; 147:7; Isaiah 12:5), and 24 for the Future (Judges 5:3; 2 Samuel 22:50; Psalm 7:17; 9:2; 18:49; 21:13; 27:6; 30:12; 57:7,9; 59:17; 61:8; 66:4 [two times]; 71:22,23; 75:9; 101:1; 104:33; 108:1,3; 138:1; 144:9; 146:2; 149:3). That's a total of 45 occurrences of *zamar* in the Old Testament (in the Piel). How did Wigram translate *zamar* in all these passages? "To play"? "To play musical instruments"? Hardly. He rendered *zamar* "sing praise" (8 times), "sing praises" (20 times), "praise" (1 time), "give praise" (2 times), "sing psalms" (2 times), and "sing" (12 times). **Not once did he use the words "play" or "play musical instruments"** (1890, p. 389).

In addition to these standard Hebrew lexicons, how have the reputable translators of the English-speaking world's most scholarly translations of the Bible translated *zamar*? "To play musical instruments"? Think again. Of the 45 occurrences of the word in the Hebrew Old Testament, the translations overwhelmingly render it "sing praise(s)" [For the listing, see Appendix A]. Other renderings include simply "sing," "praise," and "sing psalms." Rare renderings include "make melody," "make music," and "praise in psalms." Of the 10 most widely used English translations examined, including the Catholic and Jewish Bibles, only the RSV and the ESV rendered the term "play"—and then **only once** (in Psalm 144:9). It is particularly telling that, with the Old Testament written in Hebrew, Harkavy's **Jewish** Bible never once translates *zamar* "to play" or "to play an instrument." Instead, it renders the term "sing praises(s)" 28 times, "sing" 12 times, "sing psalms" 2 times, "give praise" 2 times, and "praise" 1 time. Even the *Jewish New Testament*, designed by Messianic Jew Dr. David Stern to express the "original and essential Jewishness" of the New Testament (1995, p. ix), translated Romans 15:9 to the exclusion of instrumental music: "Because of this I will acknowledge you among the Gentiles and **sing praise** to your name" (p. 217, emp. added). And how does the translation of the Septuagint (which, again, Rick agrees was the Bible of the early Christians) handle Psalm 18:49? "Therefore I will confess to thee, O Lord, among the Gentiles, and **sing** to thy name" (p. 708, emp. added).

What about the foremost biblical commentators and Hebrew dictionaries? In the article on *zamar* in the *New International Dictionary of Old Testament Theology and Exegesis*, edited by Willem VanGemeren, Leslie Allen defines the term in the Piel in the Old Testament "make music, sing praise" (1997, 1:1116). He then gives instances of playing musical instruments, but adds: "More often it has the developed sense of singing to a musical accompaniment" (1:1116). Observe the shift from playing to singing while playing. For related New Testament ideas, this dictionary points the reader to Colin Brown's *New International Dictionary of New Testament Theology* (which will be seen below to document the New Testament meaning of **sing**) and the related terms "praising, singing, thanksgiving" (1:1117; cf. 5:147). In the "Index of Semantic Fields," this dictionary lists *zamar* among the words for "singing" (5:175).

Karl Barth represents a departure from the bulk of Hebrew scholarship when he insists that *zamar* "is used in OT Hebrew solely in the sense 'sing praises (accompanied by stringed instruments)'" (1980, 4:98). Yet even he acknowledges that in the Psalms the rendering "sing praises" is more common than an instrumental understanding, and he further insists that "[t]he summons to sing Yahweh's praises to the accompaniment of strings" is a "mandate" that can no more be "delegated to professional singers **or musicians** than in the case of the summons to praise, glorify, sing, etc." (4:98, emp. added).

The culmination of current evangelical scholarship is reflected in *The Expositor's Bible Commentary* edited by the late Frank Gaebelein. The volume on the Psalms endorses the NIV rendering: "Therefore I will praise you among the nations, O Lord; I will **sing praises** to your name" (VanGemeren, 1991, 5:177, emp. added). H.C. Leupold has "Therefore will

I give thanks unto Thee among the gentiles, O Lord; And I will **sing praise** unto Thy name" (1959, p. 173, emp. added). Joseph Alexander has "Therefore I will thank thee among the nations, O Jehovah, and to thy name **will sing** (1873, p. 86, emp. added). Albert Barnes has "Therefore will I give thanks unto Thee, O Lord, among the heathen, and **sing praises** unto thy name" (1847a, 1:164, emp. added). Keil and Delitzsch have "Therefore will I praise Thee among the nations, O Jahve, And I will **sing praises** unto Thy name" (1976a, 5:249, emp. added). The same may be said for Clarke (n.d., 3:278), and the list goes on.

To summarize, here is Rick's argument in syllogistic form:

1. Paul quoted Psalm 18:49 in Romans 15:9, using *psallo* as the Greek translation of the underlying Old Testament Hebrew term *zamar*.

2. *Zamar* in the Old Testament includes the use of instrumental music.

3. Therefore, Romans 15:9 authorizes the use of instrumental music in Christian worship.

In addition to showing that Rick's assertion violates the context of Romans 15, the above linguistic data prove that neither the world's premiere Hebrew lexicographers, nor the Septuagint, nor the world's standard English translations, nor highly-respected commentators support Rick's contention. Rick's allegation that the scholarly world is in conflict with churches of Christ on whether *zamar* refers to the use of instruments is untrue. **Rick has set himself against the world's linguistic scholarship.**

Human Inference and Deduction

Rick segues from his Old Testament arguments to his New Testament arguments by making the following assertion: "If God's attitude toward instrumental music changed in the New Testament, you would expect one of the following three things: (1) a clear passage condemning its use, (2) a clear passage commanding *a cappella* praise only, or (3) a prophecy announcing the end of instrumental music." But observe that the assumption that lies behind this claim is that if God commanded the Jews or the Gentiles to practice a particular action, that action would inevitably be carried over into Christianity unless specifically forbidden. But this assumption and these criteria are manmade, arbitrary, and the result of unwarranted human expectation. Using Rick's own test, "where is the clear command of God" for these three criteria? Rick does what he condemns in others: binds his human deductions.

The only way to know what God would have Christians to do is to go to the New Testament and see what He says. Rick's approach is to go to what God told the Jews or Gentiles to do, and then insist, "Now I'm going to do what **they** did, unless God tells me otherwise." That approach is faulty and unbiblical. Further, to see the inconsistency of such thinking, simply apply Rick's criteria to other practices. Consider that there is no clear passage in the New Testament condemning the burning of incense, no clear passage commanding an alternative to the exclusion of burning incense, and no prophecy announcing the end of burning incense. There is no clear passage in the New Testament condemning infant inclusion in the covenant, no clear passage commanding adult inclusion **only**, and no prophecy announcing the end of infant inclusion. Where is the New Testament passage condemning sprinkling for baptism, or commanding immersion **only**, or prophesying the end of Mosaic sprinkling?

"New Testament Reasons for Accepting Instrumental Praise"

Next, Rick advanced five reasons from the New Testament to justify the addition of the instrument:

I. Jesus Did Not Address

Rick asserts: "Jesus never deals with the issue. The anti-instrument advocates must speak where Jesus has not spoken.... He never addressed the issue of music once. And you would think He would if this was worth splitting His church over." Once again, observe the hidden, unwarranted assumption inherent in this faulty exegetical procedure: if Jesus did not address a matter, it must be that He approves it.

- Since Jesus never dealt once with the issue of whether the Pope is His vicar on Earth, speaking in His place, He must approve of the papacy.

- Since Jesus never dealt once with smoking crack cocaine, He must approve of doing so today.

- Since Jesus never dealt once with polygamy, He must approve of plural marriage today.

This entire line of reasoning is based on the idea that silence is necessarily permissive—a faulty hermeneutical principle if there ever was one. But being "silent where the Bible is silent" does not mean doing whatever the Bible is silent on; it means to refrain from acting in areas where the Bible is silent—where God is silent, we must remain silent. Observe carefully: God does not authorize or give His permission by what He does **not** say; He authorizes, requires, and gives permission by **what He says**.

The truth is that Jesus did not specifically address **many** matters while He was on Earth. Yet He explicitly told His apostles that He would send the Holy Spirit to them so that they would be able to present the totality of the Christian religion—including many things that Jesus did not specifically say (John 16:12-13). Paul made this very point when he contrasted his additional legislation from the Lord that supplemented that which Jesus had not specifically articulated while He was on Earth (1 Corinthians 7:10,12).

Further, note that Rick's argument applies to himself as much as it does to the "anti-instrument advocates." After all, if Jesus never dealt with the issue, then for Rick to promote the use of instruments is **to speak where Jesus has not spoken**. And since churches of Christ have flourished for centuries without using the instrument, you would think that Jesus surely would have said something on the subject if it was worth Richland Hills introducing and thereby splitting His church over it.

Prodigal's Homecoming

Appealing to the parable of the Prodigal Son and the use of instrumental music (*sumphonias*) at the homecoming reception that the father had for the son (Luke 15:25), Rick drew the following conclusion:

> And so in this powerful metaphor of a son who's come back to the people of God, who's back in the house of God, Jesus says, "They were having a party and there was a band." You'd have a hard time, based on what Jesus said, arguing He had a problem with instrumental praise.

Here, again, is an inexcusable misrepresentation of the context of a Bible passage. Rick knows that scholars have long noted that the parables of Jesus were intended to press a single main point (e.g., Fee and Stuart's chapter titled "The Parables—Do You Get the Point?", 1982, pp. 123ff.; cf. Mickelsen, 1963, pp. 224,229). The point of the three parables of Luke 15 (lost sheep, lost coin, lost boy) is articulated in verses 1-3: "Then all the tax collectors and the sinners drew near to Him to hear Him. And the Pharisees and scribes murmured, saying, 'This man receives sinners and eats with them.' So He spoke this parable to them." The point Jesus made was directed to the **Jews** due to their aversion to His efforts to reach out to those elements of Jewish society that needed to hear His message. It's application to Christians pertains to the **begrudging spirit** (manifested by the elder brother) that some have when a non-Christian comes to Christ, or a fellow Christian comes back to the church after having gone off into a decadent lifestyle (vs. 32). **The context of the parable has absolutely nothing to do with the worship of God.** Question: how in the world can a person extract from such a context the notion that Jesus intended to imply that instrumental music may be used in Christian church worship? In fact, for Rick's argument to be correct, the first three verses should have read as follows:

> Then all the tax collectors and the sinners drew near to Him to hear Him. And the Pharisees and scribes murmured, saying, "This man is **including instrumental music in worship**." So He spoke this parable to them.

Are we to conclude that the other features of the son's homecoming party are to be introduced into Christian worship as well? What about incorporating a ceremonial use of a robe, ring, and sandals (vs. 22)? What about killing the fatted calf in the assembly (vs. 23)? What about dancing in worship (vs. 25)? Observe further that the instrumental music was not directed to the father—who represents God in the parable.

The same may be said for Rick's contention that since Jesus taught regularly in the temple in the midst of instrumental praise, but didn't throw out the instrumentalists along with the money changers, He must endorse its use in Christian worship. This line of reasoning is faulty for at least two reasons: (1) such would imply that Jesus would be pleased with introducing into Christian worship all other facets of Jewish temple worship as well; and (2) it ignores the fact that Jesus lived and died under the Law of Moses, was subject to its precepts while He was on Earth (Galatians 4:4), and therefore would certainly have endorsed the use of instruments **under that system**; but such proves nothing about His attitude toward instruments in **Christian** worship.

II. "Non-Issue in Acts"?

Rick's second argument from the New Testament is: "Instrumental music is a non-issue in the book of Acts." He asserts: "We do know that the early disciples met daily in the temple courts. Apparently, they could worship in spirit and truth in the presence of instrumental music." Here is another case of sheer assumption, argument from silence, and drawing an unwarranted conclusion without adequate evidence. Is Rick implying that Christians met in the temple and **participated** in Old Testament **Jewish worship**? If so, can we do so today? Would he have us to abandon our church buildings and start attending synagogues? The truth is that Christians were **informed** regarding God's expectations for worship under Christianity (e.g., Acts 2:42)—even as Jesus predicted (John 4:23-24). They did not take their cue from temple worship.

To see the naive nature of Rick's contention, some insight into the status of the first-century temple is necessary. The Herodian temple of Jesus' day was massive and included far more than the portable Tabernacle, with its Holy of Holies and Holy place, described in the Pentateuch. Indeed, according to Heinrich Graetz, in his monumental *History of the Jews*, "[t]he whole circumference of the Temple Mount...exceeded three-quarters of a mile" (1893, 2:109). In fact, the entire area of Herod's reconstruction of the temple immediately preceding the time of Christ "was between four and five times greater than that which preceded it" (Hackett, 1870, 4:3203). Robinson observed that the "Court of the Gentiles" alone comprised a space of 14 English acres (1881, p. 879), the very existence of which, according to Edersheim, "proves that the Sanctuary was largely attended by others than Jews" (1915, 1:74). Consequently, the entire temple complex, which at the time of Christ had been under virtually constant construction for 46 years (John 2:20), consisted of numerous precincts, porches, porticos, courtyards, compartments, cloisters, rooms, shops, terraces, and chambers (see McClintock and Strong, 1881, 10:258-265; cf. Lightfoot, 1859, 1:63ff.). Multiple "buildings" had been built (Matthew 24:1), including even facilities and space for both the sale and slaughter of sacrificial animals (Westerholm, 1988, 4:766; cf. Matthew 21:12; John 2:14). After a detailed and lengthy description of the temple, Edersheim confessed: "Nor does all this convey an adequate idea of **the vastness** of the Temple-buildings" (1915, 1:246, emp. added). McClintock and Strong spoke of "the **thousands** who were frequently assembled within the precincts of the courts; which also were **sometimes used for popular meetings**" (10:252, emp. added)—as much as 210,000 persons all at the same time (Edersheim, 1874, p. 69). Such numbers provided ready candidates for hearing the Gospel. Edersheim provides an excellent description of temple activity that enables the modern reader to have a more accurate sense of temple life:

> First and foremost was the great transformation in the Temple itself, which, from a small building, little larger than an ordinary church in the time of Solomon, had become that great and glorious House which excited the admiration of the foreigner, and kindled the enthusiasm of every son of Israel. At the time of Christ it had been already forty-six years in building, and workmen were still, and for a long time, engaged on it. But what **a heterogeneous crowd thronged its porches and courts!** Hellenists; scattered wanderers from the most distant parts of the earth—east, west, north, and south; Galileans, quick of temper and uncouth of Jewish speech; Judaeans and Jerusalemites; white-robed Priests and Levites; Temple officials; broad-phylacteried, wide-fringed Pharisees, and courtly, ironical Sadducees; and, in the outer court, curious Gentiles! Some had come to worship; others to pay vows, or bring offerings, or to seek purification; **some to meet friends, and discourse on religious subjects** in those colonnaded porches, which ran round the Sanctuary; or else **to have their questions answered,**

or their causes heard and decided, by the smaller Sanhedrin of twenty-three, that sat in the entering of the gate, or by the Great Sanhedrin. The latter no longer occupied the Hall of Hewn Stones, Gazith, but **met in some chamber attached to those 'shops,' or booths, on the Temple Mount**, which belonged to the High-Priestly family of Ananias, and where such profitable trade was driven by those who, in their cupidity and covetousness, were worthy successors of the sons of Eli. In the **Court of the Gentiles (or in its porches)** sat the official money-changers, who for a fixed discount changed all foreign coins into those of the Sanctuary. Here also was **that great mart for sacrificial animals**, and all that was requisite for offerings.... Here also there lay about **a crowd of noisy beggars**, unsightly from disease, and clamorous for help. And close by passed the luxurious scion of the High-Priestly families; the proud, intensely self-conscious Teacher of the Law, respectfully followed by his disciples; and the quick-witted, subtle Scribe. These were the men who, on Sabbaths and feast-days, **would come out on the Temple-terrace to teach the people, or condescend to answer their questions**; who in the Synagogues would hold their puzzled hearers spell-bound by their traditional lore and subtle argumentation (1915, pp. 114-115, parentheses in orig., emp. added).

Glimpses of this diversified (non-worship) temple activity surface in the gospel accounts themselves. For example, "the blind and the lame came to Him [Jesus—DM] **in the temple**, and He healed them" (Matthew 21:14, emp. added). Question: Did Jesus conduct a healing **worship** service, complete with instrumental music, simply because the text states that He performed healings "in the temple"? Of course not. So to claim that since early Christians met in the temple courts, they must have participated in worship that included instruments is a baseless, unproven assumption. The musical part of the Jewish service was conducted by the Levites and confined to a very specific, isolated location (Edersheim, 1915, 1:245). Even if the temple use of musical instruments could be heard in the environs, Christian worship would not have been affected by them anymore than noises in the streets surrounding our church buildings affect our worship. Many spaces were available in the temple courts where early Christians could worship together, shielded from the Romans, and exempt from interference by hostile Jews. Is Rick prepared to contend that all who entered the temple courts—many of whom were neither Jews nor Christians—were there to worship?

The New Testament itself confirms these historical facts. Read carefully the verses that allude to early Christians appearing in the vicinity of the temple: Acts 2:46; 3:2,8; 5:12,20,21,25,42. Since we know they could not have been engaging legitimately in the "obsolete" (Hebrews 8:13) worship of Judaism, why were they there? To worship with instruments? Where is the evidence for such a leap? Instead, what we do find is that they were there primarily **to impart instruction** (i.e., indoctrinate the neophyte church and evangelize non-Christian Jews). The Gospel was to go to the Jews **first** (Acts 3:26; 13:46; Romans 1:16). Religious Jews provided the most logical target audience for the new religion of the Christ—and initial contact with them could most readily occur in association with the focal point of Jewish religion, the temple. Hence, in passage after passage, indication is given that the apostles and early church were in the temple courts for indoctrination—**to educate** the new church and **to make more converts among the Jews**.

The early church was merely perpetuating the practice of Jesus Who used the temple as the central contact point for His evangelism. Jesus said He "was daily...in the temple **teaching**" (Mark 14:49, emp. added; cf. Luke 2:46). "And He was **teaching daily** in the temple. But the chief priests, the scribes, and the leaders of the people sought to destroy Him, and were unable to do anything; for **all the people** were very attentive to hear Him" (Luke 19:47-48, emp. added). "[I]n

the daytime He was teaching in the temple, but **at night** He went out and stayed on the mountain called Olivet. Then **early in the morning** all the people came to Him **in the temple to hear Him**" (Luke 21:37-38, emp. added). In addition, the first church of Christ certainly had no church building; so, as McGarvey observes, "No other place inside the city walls could have afforded room for the assemblage of such multitudes" (1892, 1:48-49).

Examine the allusions to the temple in the book of Acts and one will find the following:

- **Acts 2:** Verse 46 says they were in the temple courts. But verse 43 says the apostles performed signs and wonders. Why? To confirm the Word (Mark 16:20; Hebrews 2:3-4). So **preaching** was taking place, accompanied by the authenticating power of miracles. No worship with instruments here.

- **Acts 3:** Verse 1 says that "Peter and John were going up to the temple at the time of prayer." Observe that Luke did not say that Peter and John went up to the temple "to pray" or "to worship" (let alone with instruments!). The rest of the chapter must clarify precisely why they went to the temple at the time of Jewish prayer. Their visit would have been the very best time to present the Gospel, since (1) that's when a large number of Jews came to the temple for the evening burning of incense (cf. Luke 1:10); and (2) the catalyst for getting their attention and gaining a hearing (i.e., the lame man) was well-known to them since they would have seen him **daily** (vs. 2) lying at the popular entrance gate ("Beautiful"—vs. 2), and they would have known that he was cripple **from birth** (vs. 2). As calculated, the healing elicited interest from "all the people" (3:11), causing them to listen to Peter's sermon (vss. 12ff.). The location for this teaching, identified as Solomon's

"Porch" or "Colonnade," described in detail by Josephus and recounted by McGarvey, consisted of cloisters that were so massive in size that

> [t]hey contained space sufficient for the great multitude of the disciples when assembled in one mass; and also for many separate meetings of large numbers to listen to different preachers speaking at the same time. All the twelve apostles might be preaching in them at the same hour, each to a large audience, and yet be far enough apart to avoid confusion of sound (1892, 1:52).

Observe, then, that this historical setting lends no credence to the claim that the church incorporated instruments of music in their worship simply because they visited the temple.

- **Acts 5:** Verse 12 indicates that the evangelistic activities of the apostles, accompanied by confirming miracles, continued to be conducted in open, public areas of the temple. The inclusion of women in verse 14 suggests that these events were not specifically connected with Jewish worship (and instrumental music), since women were restricted from going beyond the Court of the Women and their participation in worship was limited (Peloubet, 1947, p. 679; Edwards, 1988, 4:1093). Verse 20 further indicates that their purpose for going to the temple courts was to "tell the people the full message of this new life" (cf. vs. 25). Luke's summary of their connection to the temple is simple: "Day after day, in the temple courts and from house to house, they never stopped teaching and proclaiming the good news that Jesus is the Christ" (vs. 42). The preaching took place **daily** in the open courts to which all Jews had legal access, as well as in the homes of those non-Christian Jews who desired to hear more. No worship with instruments here.

To summarize, observe that Rick's claim that, by visiting the temple courts, early Christians could worship in spirit and truth in the presence of instrumental music is speculation and reflects a lack of knowledge about the temple courts. Has he even considered the fact that the synagogues and temple courts would have been filled with hostile Jews who had clamored for the death of Christ? So if Christians could participate in Jewish instrumental worship in the temple, I suppose they could participate in worship with infidel Jews who rejected the deity of Christ? That hardly would be **Christian** worship.

"No Authority for Congregational Singing"?

Rick then makes a bold statement: "But no where in Acts is a pattern for musical praise specified. In fact, no where in the New Testament is congregational singing specifically authorized. Now you heard me, let me say that again. No where in the New Testament is congregational singing specifically authorized." This novel assessment of the biblical text is a **recent** assertion in the long-standing discussion of instrumental music, having been advanced by Don DeWelt in a "Letter to the Editor" in the *Gospel Advocate* on May 16, 1985. His contention: "There is no command, apostolic example or necessary inference in the New Testament for congregational singing with or without an instrument!" (127[10]:293). If that actually were the case, then why would anyone presume to worship God **in song**? What right would anyone have to do so? If God has not indicated His desire that our worship of Him include singing, such singing would be mere **human** invention. And if God accepts mere human invention/inclination for worship, then a person can worship God **any way he chooses**—no matter how bizarre or outlandish—as long as he/she is sincere. Will Rick say that God would be pleased with bringing to the assembly chirping canaries and barking dogs? May a NASCAR fan bring an engine to rev in worship? What about snake handlers—

whose sincerity cannot be questioned since many of them have died from snakebite? The "sincerity only/no authority needed" approach to worship flaunts the biblical principle of authority and throws open the doors of innovation to allow any and every artifice and whim of man—as long as he or she is "sincere." When has God ever allowed man to decide how He is to be worshipped?

By declaring that the New Testament no where authorizes congregational singing, Rick has set himself against the bulk of Christendom and the world's foremost scholars of the last two millennia, from the early "church fathers" to ecclesiastical historians and ancient commentators, not to mention the grammar of the relevant passages. McClintock and Strong provide a sweeping historical summary of the long-recognized role of **congregational** singing in Christian worship:

> The praises of God may be sung privately in the family, **but chiefly in the house of God.... From the apostolic age singing was always a part of divine service, in which the whole body of the Church joined together**; and it was the decay of this practice that first brought the order of singers into the Church. The Council of Laodicea (canon 15) prohibited singing by the congregation, designed only to restore and revive the ancient psalmody. We find that in after-ages the people enjoyed their **ancient** privilege of **singing all together** (1880, 9:776, emp. added).

Ferguson surveys the literature of Christian and non-Christian writers of the first three centuries of Christianity and demonstrates not only that instrumental music in worship was unknown, but that congregational singing characterized the churches (1971, pp. 81ff., 156ff.). As one example, Ignatius (who lived around A.D. 110) speaks of the participation of the whole congregation in singing to God through Christ (as quoted in Ferguson, p. 156).

Referring specifically to *psallontes* in Ephesians 5:19, the *Exegetical Dictionary of the New Testament* observes: "**Church members are united** through songs of thanksgiving.... This refers to 'singing aloud' (cf. 1 Cor 14:26) and **collective singing in the assembly** (Balz and Schneider, 1993, 3:495, emp. added). [NOTE: Proof that the New Testament **does** authorize and require congregational singing—explicitly and forthrightly—is given below.]

III. Not Prohibited?

Rick's third New Testament argument states: "New Testament commands to sing neither prescribe nor prohibit instrumental music." This line of thinking is also nonsensical. Consider these parallel statements:

> "New Testament commands to **eat bread** at the Lord's Table neither prescribe nor prohibit eating hamburgers."

> "New Testament commands to **drink grape juice** at the Lord's Table neither prescribe nor prohibit drinking Mountain Dew©."

> "New Testament commands to **pray** neither prescribe nor prohibit instrumental music."

> "New Testament commands to **eat the Lord's Supper** neither prescribe nor prohibit instrumental music."

The point is that New Testament commands **to pray** authorize the worshipper **to pray**. New Testament commands **to sing** authorize the worshipper **to sing**. That is precisely why New Testament Christians sing, pray, and take the Lord's Supper—because the New Testament gives commands to do so. But where in the New Testament is the command to play an instrument in worship to God? **It is not there!** Instruments are prohibited in worship—not because the command to sing includes or excludes them—but because **there are no New Testament passages that enjoin them**.

Rick's own argument is self-defeating. He insists: "New Testament **commands to sing** neither prescribe nor prohibit instrumental music." Inherent in that statement is the admission that the New Testament commands singing. That's **why** he sings. So where are the New Testament commands that prescribe **playing**? They do not exist.

Rick maintains that Ephesians 5:19, Colossians 3:16, and James 5:13 all speak to the individual, referring to the Christian's daily walk, and so, contextually, have nothing to do with the corporate assembly of the church. Question: In discussing in Ephesians how to live the Christian life 24-7, would one expect Paul to include features of the Sunday worship assembly as one aspect of the Christian walk? Could Paul, in fact, in describing how to walk worthy of the Christian calling (4:1), include proper conduct of the Christian in **both** daily, private life as well as in the corporate worship assembly of the church? Of course he could—**and he did!** The contexts and grammatical features of Ephesians 5:19 and Colossians 3:16 verify the fact that Paul (by inspiration of the Holy Spirit) framed his remarks with **the assembly** in mind. [NOTE: The reader is asked to exercise patience in considering this somewhat technical treatment, made necessary by Rick's allegations]:

1. Paul used five plural, present imperative, coordinate participles in Ephesians 5:19-21 (i.e., "speaking," "singing," "making melody," "giving thanks," "submitting"), and three such participles in Colossians 3:16 ("teaching," "admonishing," "singing") to refer to actions that may be performed at the same time by the entire congregation in order to fulfill the commands "be filled with the Spirit" (Ephesians 5:18) and "let the word of Christ dwell" (Colossians 3:16). The **plural** participles indicate Paul was speaking to the entire church collectively. The "speaking," "teaching," "making melody," "giving thanks," "submitting," and "admonishing" all occur coordinately in the process of singing.

2. The reflexive pronoun in Ephesians 5:19 (*heautois*) and Colossians 3:16 (*heautous*), translated "one another," is used **reciprocally** to indicate that those assembled perform the activity **together**. Greek authorities are definitive on this point. For example, in defining the nature of reciprocity, Summers explains: "In function it represents an **interchange of action** between **the members of a plural subject**" (Summers, 1950, p. 120; emp. added). But the plural subject to which Paul directed his remarks in both Ephesians and Colossians is the church. The members are the plural subject between whom the interchange of action (singing) was to occur. Hence, the singing in those two passages refers to **congregational** singing. A.T. Robertson states that this reciprocal usage "brings out the **mutual relations** involved" (1934, p. 692, emp. added). Hanna observes that "the exhortation seems to be given to **a corporate group of believers**" (1983, p. 373, emp. added). H.K. Bartels explains: "H. Schlier is doubtless correct in seeing that Eph. 5:18ff. and Col. 3:16 presuppose a situation similar to that in 1 Cor. 14:15, i.e., **the regular worship of the early Christian community**" (1978, 3:675, emp. added). Lightfoot insists: "The reciprocal *heauton* differs from the reciprocal *allelon* in emphasizing **the idea of corporate unity**" (1875, p. 287; cf. Moulton & Milligan, 1930, p. 177). Abbott agrees that it "is true, that *heautois* suggests, more than *allelois*, that they are addressed as members of **one corporate body**. This use of the word is quite classical" (1897, p. 145, emp. added). Nicoll also agrees: "If there is any distinction between them, it is that the idea of **fellowship or corporate unity** is more prominent in *heautois*" (n.d., 3:349, emp. added). Schlier notes that the word for "songs" in Ephesians 5:19 and Colossians 3:16 refers to songs that "are **not** sung by the individual, but by **the community gathered for worship**" (1964, 1:164, emp. added). Many other Greek authorities verify these same observations, including: Smith, 1937, pp. 121,126; Chamberlain, 1941, p. 52; Harper

& Weidner, 1888, p. 433; Arndt & Gingrich, 1957, pp. 38,211; Thayer, 1901, p. 163; Machen, 1923, p. 154; Robinson, 1879, p. 199; Blass & Debrunner, 1961, p. 150; Dana & Mantey, 1927, p. 131; Kuhner, 1853, p. 455; et al.

3. The phrase "in you" (*en humin*) in Colossians 3:16 is the favorite expression used by Paul to refer to **the church assembly**: 1 Corinthians 1:10,11; 2:2; 3:3,16,18; 5:1; 6:5; 11:18,19,30; 14:25; 15:12; Colossians 4:16 (Delling, 1972, 8:498).

4. Paul contrasted their **assembly** with his absence **from that assembly**: "For though I am absent **from you** in body, I am present **with you** in spirit and delight to see how orderly you are and how firm your faith in Christ is" (Colossians 2:5, emp. added). He was not referring to his absence from each of their individual homes; he was referring to his absence from their collective assembly.

5. Paul called for the Colossian and Laodicean letters to be read aloud "in the church," i.e., **in the assembly** (Colossians 4:16).

6. The context of Ephesians 5:18 pertains to the debauchery of pagan temple worship as contrasted with **the worship of the Christian church**:

> Throughout the whole passage there is a contrast implied between the Heathen and the Christian practice, q.d. *When you meet, let your enjoyment consist, not in fulness of wine, but fulness of the Spirit; let your songs be, not the drinking-songs of heathen feasts, but psalms and hymns; and their accompaniment,* **not the music of the lyre, but the melody of the heart;** *while you sing them in praise, not of Bacchus or Venus, but of the Lord Jesus Christ* (Conybeare and Howson, 1899, p. 775, italics in orig., emp. added; cf. p. 760).

Summarizing, while Ephesians and Colossians certainly include much material that pertains to everyday Christian living, they also contain directives that relate specifically to **the church**

worship assembly. The grammatical features selected by the Holy Spirit in the wording of Ephesians 5:19 and Colossians 3:16 demonstrate that congregational singing is under discussion. **Rick pits himself against the world's scholarship on this point as well.**

"Only Solos in the Assembly"?

Rick also makes the following assertion:

Here's the irony. There's only one reference I know of in the entire New Testament to music in the assembly. It's in 1 Corinthians 14:26.... Now here's the point. The only reference to music in the assembly in the New Testament is talking about solos.... Isn't it ironic the only music mentioned specifically in the assembly in the New Testament is solos, which I guarantee you are forbidden in churches that have the anti-instrument position.

Two observations:

1. Rick could not prove that "each of you has a psalm" in 1 Corinthians 14:26 refers to the singing of **solos** if his life depended on it. The evidence, in fact, points away from that conclusion: (a) Paul just as certainly could have been referring to **inspired song leaders** who were motivated by the Spirit to lead the congregation in particular songs, but who, like the tongue-speakers and prophets (vss. 27-32), were spontaneously interfering with each other's actions; (b) Paul could have been referring to individuals whom the Holy Spirit moved to **recite (not sing) an inspired psalm (poem)** for the enrichment of the congregation—either one from the Old Testament Psalms that the individual did not need to consult, or a newly inspired psalm given by God for the first time. The modern parallel would be our oral Scripture readings in the assembly; (c) "Each of you has a psalm" may very well be a reference to inspired hymn **writers** who **taught the congregation** new songs for the congregation to sing. After all, the infant church did not

have *Praise for the Lord* or any of the other hymnals so readily available to the church today. Those initial churches would have been in as much need of suitable songs for the assembly as they were in need of inspired instruction on other aspects of worship via prophecy, tongue-speaking, etc. (cf. McClintock & Strong, 1880, 6:757).

To conclude that "each of you has a psalm" refers to solo-singing is, in Rick's own words, "standing **over** the Word of God." The text does not say, "Each of you has a solo." A "psalm" is not a solo; it is an inspired **poem** that may be sung **or** read. The highly respected 17th century Hebraist J.B. Lightfoot published a commentary on the New Testament incorporating his vast grasp of Hebrew and Aramaic usage, including the Jewish Talmud and Mishna. His understanding of the meaning of *psalmos* in 1 Corinthians 14:26 entailed congregational singing, as reflected in his paraphrase of the verse: "**When ye come together into one place**, one is for having the time and worship spent chiefly in **singing psalms**, another in preaching, &c. One prefers **singing of psalms**, another a tongue, another preaching" (1859, 4:266, emp. added).

2. More germane to the matter of instrumental music, notice that Rick admits that 1 Corinthians 14:26 refers to **singing in the assembly**. This admission is also inherent in his third argument from the New Testament: "New Testament **commands to sing** neither prescribe nor prohibit instrumental music." So if Rick were to remain **biblical**, and confine himself to **what the New Testament says**, he would limit the musical aspect of assembly worship to **singing** (albeit, in his mind, solo-singing). If only one passage in the New Testament (according to Rick) refers to what is to be done in the assembly of the church as it relates to music, and if that one passage refers solely to singing—not playing instruments—by what authority do Rick and Richland Hills "go beyond what is written" (1

Corinthians 4:6) by introducing instrumental music into their worship assembly?

Observe further that when Rick asserts that "these passages are talking about our **lifestyle**," not only is he unbiblically redefining "lifestyle" to **exclude** assembly worship behavior, he also implies that the New Testament has **nothing** to say about assembly worship. Question: Did God leave the issue of music in assembly worship completely unaddressed and unregulated? If so, why have **any** music whatsoever—whether vocal or instrumental or both? Instead of singing, why not limit all worship in the assembly to whistling? Or yodeling? Or humming? Why does Richland Hills even have an assembly? Why do they take up a collection of money? Why do they offer the Lord's Supper? The only legitimate answer to these questions is that the New Testament depicts first-century Christians conducting themselves in harmony with apostolic instruction, and therefore we are **obligated** to do the same. We should sing because the three passages in the New Testament that address assembly music (i.e., 1 Corinthians 14:15,26; Ephesians 5:19; Colossians 3:16) indicate that the first-century church met together and sang spiritual songs. Neither those passages, nor any others, indicate that the first-century church whistled, yodeled, or played instruments in worship to God. It's that simple—and that **certain**.

"No Command to Sing <u>Only?</u>"

Rick also notes that "[t]here is no New Testament command to sing **only** *a cappella*. To say that 'sing' means 'sing **only**' is a human inference that comes dangerously close to speaking where God has not spoken." Agreed. But that misses the point. We sing because the New Testament tells us to sing. The New Testament does not tell us to play instruments. So, if the New Testament does not say to "play an instrument," yet Rick and Richland Hills have introduced instruments, by his own admission, "that comes dangerously close to speaking where God has not spoken." In fact, they're not merely "close," they're there. They have spoken, and are now practicing, that which God has not spoken or sanctioned. Rick asks, "Can we honestly say that the early Christians, especially in view of their knowledge of the Old Testament, would have concluded that 'sing' means 'sing unaccompanied'?" The answer is a resounding, "Yes!" As will be shown, the testimony of early church history verifies that very fact. To assert otherwise is sheer assertion—not proof.

Rick then affirms: "Please understand nobody's arguing, and nobody has ever argued, that we should replace singing with playing. We're simply saying that the one does not preclude or forbid the other." Again, I agree. The command to "sing" does not preclude or forbid "playing," and the command to "play" does not preclude or forbid "singing." So where is the biblical justification for doing either one? In his desire to maintain some semblance of attachment to Scripture, he freely concedes that singing is fine. Why? Because singing is included in New Testament allusions to worship. But by insisting that those verses do not say "sing **only**," and that adding "playing" does not exclude "singing," Rick has undercut the only legitimate means for ascertaining what God would have us to do in worship.

If God had decided to restrict Christian worship to playing instruments, what would we expect Him to have said? Answer: He would have told Christians to play instruments in worship to Him. If God had decided to have Christians worship Him by **both** singing **and** playing instruments, what would we expect Him to have said? Answer: He would have told Christians to sing **and** play. If God had decided to restrict Christian worship to singing, what would we expect Him to have said? Answer: Precisely what He said! "Sing." But that's not good enough for Rick; he insists that God should have said "sing

only." To quote Rick, I ask you, "Is that standing **under** the Word of God, or **over** it?"

Rick's final point under New Testament argument #III is: "Where is the specific word anywhere in the Bible that forbids what in the Old Testament is called 'with one voice' the singing and playing of praise given to God?" As previously noted, this biased perspective imposes an unwarranted human assumption on the text. Parallels expose the fallacy: Where is the specific word anywhere in the Bible that forbids what in the Old Testament is called "an aroma pleasing to the Lord" in the animal, grain, and liquid offerings? The fact is that the vast majority of the things forbidden to Christians, both in and out of worship, are not explicitly/specifically forbidden, but are only forbidden by implication and principle. Where is the specific word anywhere in the Bible that forbids polygamy? Must we have such a prohibition to know that God is not pleased with polygamy? Must the Bible specifically say, "monogamy **only**"? If Rick was consistent, he would approve of polygamy and perhaps have two or more wives like the Quran teaches (*Surah* 4:3).

IV. In Heaven?

Rick's fourth argument is as follows: "The New Testament refers to instrumental music in heaven." His proof for this contention is Revelation 5:8 and 15:2-3. After reading these passages, Rick makes an impassioned rebuttal to those who insist that Revelation is figurative and the instruments mentioned in Revelation are not literal:

> I argue that whether it's literal or figurative is irrelevant. The Revelation was written to a persecuted church dying for the faith, and these early Christians are wondering is Jesus and the gospel worth hanging on to, and John says, "Here's an image from heaven, here's a spirit-given image for you to realize that the saints that died for the faith, the saints that are martyred for the faith, they're around the throne of God

46

now playing and singing His praise. You see that picture and you hold onto your faith." It served the eternal purpose of God for that figure to bless those Christians.... Am I honestly to believe that what God is enjoying right now in heaven, He is despising on earth?"

Rick has side-stepped the point completely. If the images and figures of Revelation are symbolic, then God is **not** "enjoying right now in heaven" instrumental music. Does Rick honestly believe that God (Who is spirit—John 4:24), or anyone else in heaven, is actually holding and playing **literal, physical instruments of music**? Perhaps they are driving BMWs on the "street of...gold" (Revelation 21:21). Will Stradivarius be there to construct one of his world famous violins? Will a kennel of cats be there to provide the raw material for the strings? Such literalisms are ludicrous and cheapen the eternal realm. No such physical accoutrements will exist in heaven. Heaven is a **spiritual** realm inhabited by **spirit** beings (cf. 1 Corinthians 15:50; Hebrews 12:23).

The book of Revelation goes out of its way to help the reader avoid the very mistake that Rick makes. It repeatedly gives indication that its images are purely figurative and symbolic and not to be taken literally—including its numbers, objects, locations, animals, etc. The word translated "revelation" in the very first verse (1:1—*apocalupsis*) refers to literature that is cryptic, non-literal, and figurative. In addition to using weird, outlandish images, like seven-headed beasts (13:1) and locusts with scorpion stingers (9:10) to underscore the deliberate exaggeration being employed, the text occasionally tips the reader off to the precise meaning of an image. For example, we are informed that the seven stars in the right hand of Jesus symbolize the seven angels/messengers of the churches and that the lampstands represent the churches (1:20). The seven-headed, blood-red dragon symbolizes Satan (12:9). The "many waters" on which the great prostitute sits represents peoples and nations (17:15). Notice that a dragon is not Satan, and Satan is not a literal dragon. An olive oil lampstand is not a church, and a church is not a literal lampstand. Waters are not people, and people are not literally water.

It so happens that one of those times when the Holy Spirit divulged the meaning of some of the imagery is in one of the very passages on which Rick stakes his case:

> Then I saw a Lamb, looking as if it had been slain, standing in the center of the throne, encircled by the four living creatures and the elders. He had seven horns and seven eyes, which are the seven spirits of God sent out into all the earth. He came and took the scroll from the right hand of him who sat on the throne. And when he had taken it, the four living creatures and the twenty-four elders fell down before the Lamb. Each one had a harp and they were holding golden bowls full of incense, **which are the prayers of the saints** (Revelation 5:6-8, emp. added).

This great section of the Revelation alludes to Jesus—the Lamb slain on our behalf. He is depicted as having seven horns and seven eyes. If you and I could see Jesus right now in His heavenly state, would He have seven horns and seven eyes? After all, that image is a "Spirit-given image." Are there seven spirits of God—or only one Spirit represented by the perfect number seven? Answer: There is only one Holy Spirit (Ephesians 4:4). Did God hold a literal scroll in His right hand? No. Do the four living creatures (see their description in Revelation 4:6-8) and 24 elders actually exist? No, they are purely symbolic—and a symbol does not symbolize itself. We are specifically told that the golden bowls of incense "are the prayers of the saints" (5:9). Are bowls actually prayers, or are prayers literally bowls? Of course not. Then why on Earth would anyone wish to take the phrase "each one had a harp" and conclude that saints are actually playing literal harps in heaven in the presence of God? Answer: Only those who are grasping for any possible straw to justify what they have pre-decided to do—only those who are standing **over** the Word of God rather than **under** it. Likewise, in Revelation 15, the harps are no more literal than the other images mentioned in the context—the seven plagues and the sea of glass mingled with fire.

What's more, even if physical instruments of music were utilized in heaven, their use would not be justified in the New Testament church. If what is done in heaven may be done in the church now, will we do in heaven what is done in the church now? Will we partake of the Lord's Supper and contribute financially in heaven? Of course not. Though we marry on Earth, does marriage occur in heaven? Jesus said it does not (Matthew 22:30).

A biblical parallel to this line of reasoning may be seen in God's instructions to Moses regarding the retrieval of water for the Israelites. While traveling from Egypt to Sinai, no water was available at Rephidim, so God instructed Moses to **strike** the rock (Exodus 17:5-6). Yet during the 40-year period of desert meandering, a similar incident arose when there was no water for the community at Kadesh. On that occasion, God instructed Moses to **speak** to the rock (Numbers 20:8). Yet, Moses disobeyed and struck the rock, eliciting for himself God's displeasure and a judgment sentence that banned him from entering the Promised Land (vs. 12; cf. Deuteronomy 32:51). Using Rick's reasoning, Moses should have argued with God that since He was pleased with striking the rock at Rephidim, He must surely be pleased with doing the same at Kadesh. But instead of resorting to such human reasoning, that so often gets people into trouble (e.g., 1 Samuel 15:10-23), we ought simply to acquiesce to God and comply humbly with His directives (Genesis 6:22). Neither the use of instruments in Judaism nor the use of instruments in heaven provide scriptural justification for the use of instruments in Christian worship.

V. Giftedness?

Rick's final argument is: "The New Testament idea of giftedness supports the practice of instrumental praise." Rick asks: "If God was honored by the sincere offerings of instrumentalists in the Old Testament, why would He not be now?" The obvious answer to that question is that God may choose not to be honored the same way in every period of human history. As already noted, God has enjoined differing acts of worship at different times. Burning incense and lighting olive oil lamps were appropriate under Judaism—but not under Christianity. Further, the clamor for instrumental music betrays a misunderstanding of the nature of worship and moves the worshipper away from the **spiritual** nature of worship to a more physical, fleshly emphasis. Paul pinpointed this malady among the Athenians: "God, who made the world and everything in it, since He is Lord of heaven and earth, does not dwell in temples **made with hands. Nor is He worshiped with men's hands, as though He needed anything**, since He gives to all life, breath, and all things" (Acts 17:24-25, emp. added). God does not need human hands plucking manmade contraptions in order to be honored. Worship, under the Christian era, downplays the physical in order to accentuate the spiritual (John 4:23-24).

Rick insists that use of the instrument is "not just an aid to worship, it is an act of worship." Consequently musicians, actors, and painters ought to be allowed to exercise their "gifts" to "bless the body." Certainly, the Bible teaches that human talent ought to be harnessed in service to God and fellowman (e.g., Matthew 25:14ff.). However, nowhere does the Bible teach that humans are free to employ their talents and gifts anytime or in any way they choose. Most assuredly, humans are forbidden by God to tamper with worship protocol. **God** stipulates how humans are to worship Him. Humans do not have the right to tamper with those stipulations. We must worship Him in accordance with His instructions (e.g., Leviticus 10:3; 1 Samuel 15:22; 1 Chronicles 15:13; John 4:24; Hebrews 12:28).

Rick misrepresents God on the matter of gifts. For example, he admits that instrumental music was introduced into the worship of God by David. David, however, lived some 500-600 years **after** the Law of Moses was given and Judaism commenced. That means that all the Israelites who lived from 1500 to 950 B.C., who possessed the ability to play mechanical instruments, were **denied** the right and privilege of exercising their gift in Jewish worship. And then, when God finally authorized the use of instruments in Jewish worship at the time of David, He confined the playing to **the male Levites**. What about all those Israelites who were members of the other tribes who had the ability to play instruments? Based on Rick's reasoning, God was guilty of the very wrong he indicts "anti-instrumentalists" for committing—denying the right of musicians to use their gift in worship. The anti-instrumentalists are in good company.

Question: Is Rick willing for every worshipper to employ **in the worship of God** whatever his or her particular talent or gift might be? What about hair stylists? May they set their barber chairs in the aisles of the auditorium and worship God during the assembly by cutting hair to His glory? What about grocery stockers? What about truck drivers? What about medical doctors? Let's have a brain surgeon perform surgery in the aisle or on the rostrum. Does God want these individuals to do their daily work to the best of their ability "as working for the Lord" (Colossians 3:23)? Absolutely! But **not in the worship assembly of the church**! Worship is to be focused **on God**—not the worshipper and his or her talents. Musicians have many outlets through which they can use their skills in harmony with God's will (e.g., playing secular songs for seniors in a nursing home). But to reason that such talent ought to be incorporated in the worship assembly of the church is to be guilty of corrupting the worship of God—like Cain (Genesis 4). It is standing **over** the worship of God rather than **under** it.

"Making it Difficult"?

Rick notes: "I said last week, 'Why would we make it difficult for the unbeliever who's trying to find God?' But now I ask today, 'Why would we make it difficult for our own members and our own kids, who just want to serve God with their gifts?'" Again, note the inherent assumption: the worshiper ought to be given the right to decide how to worship God, based on his or her personal talents. Here is a sad commentary on how the changes in American culture in the last half-century have infiltrated the church (see Miller, 1996). Those generations following World War 2 are characterized by their rejection of authority outside themselves. They are spoiled children who insist on having their own way. They want to pursue religion on their own terms, and they don't want anyone telling them what they can or cannot do. This entire approach to religion and worship commences at the wrong starting point. The world is asking, "How do **I** prefer to worship God? What do **I think** I should do in religion?" when they should start at Scriptures like Proverbs 1:7 and Ecclesiastes 12:13 which teach that fearing the Lord is the **beginning** of knowledge and keeping His commands is the **whole of man**. Our attitude in worship ought to be, "Lord, what would you have me to do?," rather than, "Why can't I do what I want to do by exercising my gift?" The latter smacks of pride and "self-imposed worship" (Colossians 2:23), while the former manifests humility and submission. Furthermore, when Rick says we should not make it difficult for "our own kids," is he willing to include the wide gamut of musical manifestations current in secular culture—from rap to heavy metal?

"The Authority to Forbid"?

Rick then notes: "The bottom line still remains—listen close—the authority to forbid instrumental music has got to be established apart from a clear command of God. You can't open your Bible and show me where God forbids it." This assertion subtly shifts the issue. In reality, the **true** bottom line is: "The authority to **introduce** instrumental music has got to be established apart from a clear command of God. You can't open your Bible and show me where God enjoins it." Which is the more biblical approach? Rick's "bottom line" means that our assemblies have the right to include holy water, saint worship, images, rosaries, prayer candles, incense, clerical robes, and pork barbecue on the Lord's Table—after all, "you can't open your Bible and show me where God forbids them."

Rick believes that the New Testament writers would be "appalled to learn how we have lifted their verses and made them say things that were never even remotely on their minds." I agree. They would be appalled to learn that anyone would take any verse from the New Testament and engage in a convoluted contortion in order to make it support instrumental music, as if instrumental music was even remotely on their minds.

"Connected to the Cross"?

Rick insists that use of the instrument is a non-issue because it lacks a more direct link to the central message of Christianity—the cross—which, he says, explains why baptism and communion are mentioned so prominently. But if instrumental music is such a non-issue and so detached from the cross, why does he insist on introducing it and causing division as a result? Besides, his theory is faulty: if baptism and communion are more important to God than the use or non-use of the instrument—since they are more directly connected to the cross—why does the New Testament say more about **prayer** than baptism or the Lord's

Supper? Why does it say more about **the use of our money** than baptism or the Lord's Supper? Why does it say more about miracles and reverting to Judaism? My point: far from minimizing or relegating to a "non-issue" the use or non-use of instrumental music, the centrality of Christ and the cross in the Christian message **includes and elevates** the importance of proper worship protocol. The fact that Christ died for our sins is ample reason to manifest humble reverence and loving regard for how He says He is to be worshipped. When we do precisely what Paul tells us to do in Ephesians 5:19, sing and make melody in our hearts **to the Lord**, we exalt Christ and the cross and we express our sincere gratitude for His sacrifice on the cross. To add instruments to such an event is hardly trivial. It is pretentious and divisive. The "seven ones" of Ephesians 4:4-6 most certainly include the "one Lord." But they also include the "one body" (the church) and the "one faith," which is the doctrine transmitted by Christ through His apostles—doctrine that includes **specifications regarding how to worship Him**.

Rick claims to find support for his position from Everett Ferguson's book *A Cappella Music in the Public Worship of the Church*, when it says, "Before leaving the New Testament references, we may note in passing that the New Testament gives no negative judgment on instrumental music *per se*.... The situation is simply that instruments are not referred to in the church's worship" (1972, pp. 40-41). Commenting on this quote, Rick says, "I would say 'yes,' it was a non-issue. They're not spoken about positively, they're not spoken about negatively, they're not prescribed, they're not precluded. It wasn't an issue." As noted earlier, Rick is relying on a faulty hermeneutical principle. He is assuming that if the Bible does not issue an explicit, specific negative judgment on a practice, we are free to engage in that practice. That would mean, of course, that we could use bread and water on the Lord's

Table (as the Mormons do), we could sprinkle for baptism, or we could participate in voodoo. After all, voodoo was "a non-issue" in the early church. Moreover, Rick completely misapplies the comment and misses the point that Ferguson intended to make, as is clear from Ferguson's own conclusions regarding the evidence:

> The conclusion drawn from the New Testament texts and from linguistic evidence was that **instrumental music was not present in the worship of the New Testament church**.... [T]he absence of any clear reference to instrumental music in the church's worship in early days **was not accidental. It was not mentioned because it was not there** (pp. 40,73, emp. added).

Rick neglects to divulge this clarification.

"Arguments Against Accepting Instrumental Praise to God"

Having completed his five arguments from the New Testament that purport to prove divine sanction for instrumental music, Rick next offers to respond to what he labels the two most common arguments against instrumental music:

I. The *Psallo* Argument

Rick mistakenly identifies the English word "sing" in Ephesians 5:19 with the Greek word *psallo*. But the Greek word translated "sing" in both Ephesians 5:19 and Colossians 3:16 is *adontes*. The word *psallo* does not occur in Colossians 3:16. It does occur in Ephesians 5:19, where it is translated—not "sing"—but "making melody" (KJV, NKJV, ASV, NASB, RSV) or "make music" (NIV). Rick reasons that the dominant meaning of *psallo* in the Septuagint was to pluck and then to play a stringed instrument, and that since the Bible of the first Christians was the Septuagint, they would have understood *psallo* to mean to play or to pluck. He then concludes: "But they [i.e., anti-instrumentalists—DM] argue that on the street by the first century *psallo* had evolved to include the idea of making music with the voice, and some contend it **only** meant that by the first century, and that's how Paul meant for it to be understood.... I will just tell you: the bulk of scholarship disagrees." These last five words are absolutely false. **The truth is that the bulk of scholarship disagrees with Rick's conclusion**. I can only assume that if he did not merely rely on those who claim to have done the research for him, with all the humility I can muster, my brother lacked sufficient linguistic expertise to make sense of the evidence presented in the lexical sources. Please consider carefully the following observations:

1. He ignores the fact that the early church had, in addition to the Old Testament Scriptures, the apostles and miraculous gifts that gave them immediate instruction on how to worship God—beginning on the very day the church commenced on Earth (cf. Acts 2:42). So they did not have to rely on the Septuagint to know how to worship God under New Testament Christianity.

2. He ignores the fact that though the Septuagint was used prominently by the early church, having been produced two-and-a-half centuries earlier, many of its words had changed meaning. Indeed, one of the great scholarly discoveries of the 19th century was the fact that the New Testament was written, not in classical, but in **Koine** Greek (cf. Liddell and Scott, 1843, p. x[note]; Dana and Mantey, 1927, pp. ivff.). Consequently, in the same way that the words in the 400-year-old King James Version have undergone dramatic changes in meaning, necessitating constant clarification by those who use it, so early Christians could and would have recognized the transformation in the Greek language and made adjustments accordingly. [See additional reference to the Septuagint below.]

3. He alleges that anti-instrumentalists insist that by the first century, *psallo* included the idea of singing or perhaps **only** singing. While I do not subscribe to that concept, where

56

did those who make that claim get such an idea? Rick fails to mention the fact that they derived it **from the Greek authorities themselves**. You do not have to be a Greek scholar to read the evidence for yourself. You just have to be diligent, patient, objective, and attentive.

Greek Lexical Evidence

I invite you to consider the following lexical evidence for *psallo* from the most widely recognized Greek authorities of our time. [NOTE: In these listings, I transliterate some Greek words and omit some Greek phrases, classical citations, etc. for clarity, being careful to avoid altering original intent.]

- **Thayer**: a. *to pluck off, pull out*; b. *to cause to vibrate by touching, to twang*; *to touch* or *strike the chord, to twang the strings* of a musical instrument so that they gently vibrate; and absolutely *to play on a stringed instrument, to play the harp*, etc.... **in the N.T. to sing a hymn, to celebrate the praises of God in song**, Jas. v. 13; in honor of God, Eph. v. 19; Ro. xv. 9; 'I will **sing God's praises** indeed with my whole soul stirred and borne away by the Holy Spirit, but I will also follow reason as my guide, so that what **I sing** may be understood alike by myself and by the listeners', 1 Co. xiv. 15 (1901, p. 675, emp. added, italics in orig.).

Observe that Thayer maintains that *psallo* had changed meaning by the time the New Testament was written and so referred **exclusively** to singing. He, in fact, alludes to every single verse in the New Testament where *psallo* occurs and assigns the same meaning to all of them—**to sing**. The same may be said for Thayer's definition of *psalmos*: "a striking, twanging; spec. a striking the chords of a musical instrument; **hence, a pious song, a psalm, Eph. v. 19; Col. iii. 16**; the phrase *ekein psalmon* [to have a psalm—DM] is used of one who has it in his heart **to sing or recite a song** of the sort, 1 C. xiv. 26" (p. 675, emp. added).

- **Moulton & Milligan**: properly = 'play on a harp,' **but in the NT,** as in Jas 5[13], = '**sing a hymn**' (1930, p. 697, emp. added).
- **Vine**: "PSALLO, primarily to twitch, twang, then, to play a stringed instrument with the fingers, and hence, in the Sept., to sing with a harp, sing psalms, denotes, **in the N.T., to sing a hymn, sing praise**; in Eph. 5:19, "making melody" (for the preceding word *ado*, see SING). Elsewhere it is rendered "sing," Rom. 15:9; I Cor. 14:15; in Jas. 5:13, R.V., "let him sing praise" (A.V., "let him sing psalms") (1940, p. 58, emp. added, italics and parenthetical items in orig.).
- **Perschbacher**: *to move by a touch, to twitch; to touch, strike* the strings or chords of an instrument; absolutely *to play on a stringed instrument; to sing to music*; **in N.T. *to sing praises*,** Rom. 15:9; 1 Cor. 14:15; Eph. 5:19; James 5:13 (1990, p. 442, emp. added, italics in orig.).
- **Berry**: *to sing,* accompanied with instruments, ***to sing psalms,* Ro. xv.9; I Cor. xiv.15; Ep. v.19; Ja. v.13** (1897a, p. 109, emp. added, italics in orig.).

Observe that Berry follows the same pattern as the other lexicographers by placing the meaning in italics ("to sing"), followed by a non-italicized mention of the accompaniment of instruments, followed by **the New Testament meaning** ("to sing psalms") together with the four occurrences of the word in the New Testament. This assessment is confirmed by Berry's Greek-English interlinear where he translates *psallontes* in Ephesians 5:19 as "praising" (1897b, p. 509).

- **Hickie**: *to strike* a musical instrument; *to sing hymns,* James v. 13. Ephes. v. 19. Rom. xv. 9. 1 Cor. xiv. 15 (1893, p. 211, italics in orig.).

Again, observe closely that Hickie gives the original, radical meaning of the word as "to strike"—indicated in italics, keeping "a musical instrument" non-italicized. Then he moves to the New Testament meaning of the term in italics, "to sing hymns," as indicated by the four New Testament occurrences of the word. Hickie's lexicon is included at the end of the Greek text of the New Testament produced by the renowned textual critics Westcott and Hort (1964).

- **Kubo**: [on Ephesians 5:19—DM] *psalmos*, song of praise, psalm; *psallo*, **sing, sing praise** (1975, p. 186, emp. added).

- **Bauer/Danker/Arndt/Gingrich**: in our lit., in accordance w. OT usage, **to sing songs of praise, with or without instrumental accompaniment, *sing, sing praise*** w. dat. of the one for whom the praise is intended **Ro 15:9. Eph 5:19**.... The original meaning of *psallo* was 'pluck', 'play' (a stringed instrument); this persisted at least to the time of Lucian. In the LXX (Septuagint—DM) *psallo* frequently means 'sing', whether to the accompaniment of an instrument (Ps 32:2, 97:5 al.) **or not, as is usually the case** (Ps 7:18; 9:12; 107:4 al.). This focus on singing continued until *psallo* in Mod. Gk. means 'sing' exclusively; cp. *psaltais*=singer, chanter, w. no ref. to instrumental accompaniment. Although the NT does not voice opposition to instrumental music, in view of Christian resistance to mystery cults, as well as Pharisaic aversion to musical instruments in worship, it is likely that some such sense as *make melody* is best understood in this Eph pass. Those who favor 'play' may be relying too much on the earliest mng. of *psallo*. *Psallo to pneumatic* [sing with the spirit—DM] and in contrast to that *psallo to noi* [sing with the understanding—DM] *sing praise in spiritual ecstasy* and *in full possession of one's*

> *mental faculties* **1 Cor 14:15**. Absolutely sing praise
> **Js 5:13** (Danker, 2000, p. 1096, emp., italics, and
> parenthetical items in orig.).

This last lexicon is a little more tedious to sort out, but when examined carefully, shows itself to be in complete harmony with the other lexicographers. Consider the following six observations: (1) the insertion of "with or without instrumental accompaniment" is an admission that no instrument automatically inheres in the word *psallo*. The insertion is simply an acknowledgement that the action of *psallo* can be done on an instrument, and often was in classical usage, but use of an instrument is not inherent in the term itself—even as "songs of praise" are not inherent in "sing;" (2) after this insertion and a separating comma, the words "sing, sing praise" are placed in italics (to denote a continuation of the definition) and linked with the Greek dative case as it occurs in Romans 15:9 and Ephesians 5:19—the *psallo*ing done in those two passages consists of "sing, sing praise;" (3) acknowledgement is then made regarding the gradual change in meaning that occurred—from the original meaning of "pluck/play" to "sing" in the Greek Bible, sometimes with an instrument, **but more often without it**, to modern Greek where the term means "sing" exclusively to the complete exclusion of instruments—a change that the lexicographers with almost one accord insist had occurred by the time of the New Testament; (4) the statement, "Although the NT does not voice opposition to instrumental music," is a theological (not lexical) statement that shows the authors' bias and has no connection to actual linguistic analysis; (5) yet, even then, honesty compels him to admit that "make melody" is likely intended in Ephesians 5:19 and that those who claim otherwise are relying too much on the original/radical meaning of *psallo*; and (6) the author proceeds to translate *psallo* in both 1 Corinthians 14:15 and James 5:13 as "sing praise," adding "Absolutely" to the James rendering. This lexicon offers no comfort to those who desire to use the instrument in the assembly.

Interestingly enough, in this same lexicon, the very next word listing is *psalmos*, which is defined as: "in our lit. only ***song of praise, psalm*** in accordance w. OT usage. (a) of OT Psalms. (b) of Christian songs of praise **1 Cor 14:26. Eph 5:19**; sim. **Col 3:16**" (p. 1096, emp. and italics in orig.). In his monumental *Figures of Speech Used in the Bible*, E.W. Bullinger makes the same point: "Although the first word, *psalmos*, implies musical instruments, it was only in Old Testament worship that these were used: **not in the New Testament, nor in the Primitive Church**" (1898, p. 334, emp. added, italics in orig.). No instruments are included in *psalmos*—as verified by the other lexicographers as well (Perschbacher, p. 442; Berry, p. 109; Danker, p. 1096; Thayer, p. 675; Hickie, p. 211). And in his *Shorter Lexicon of the Greek New Testament*, Gingrich defines *psallo* simply as "sing, sing praise Ro 15:9; 1 Cor 14:15; Eph 5:19; Js 5:13" (1965, p. 238). He defines *psalmos* "song of praise, psalm" (p. 238). [NOTE: Even as a theological opinion is inserted above, so an earlier edition of the Arndt and Gingrich lexicon tampers with the meaning of *psallo* by means of a parenthetical insertion, eliciting a challenge by scholars among churches of Christ that ultimately bore a measure of success. See Jackson, 1979, 121(10):152-153; Bales, 1973, pp. 114-116; McCord, 1962, 104(44):689,695; McCord, 1964, 106(34):539-540; McCord, 1990, 21(4):27-30.]

Summary of Lexical Data on *Psallo*

In case after case, lexicon after lexicon, after noting the original and root meaning of "to touch, pluck, etc.," the Greek authorities explain that **by the first century and in the New Testament, *psallo* meant "to sing."** Once again, Rick has set himself against Greek scholarship.

In addition to these lexicographers, numerous other lexicons could be cited that date back to more remote times that also reveal the transitional development of the meaning of *psallo*. Kurfees collated 17 lexicons a hundred years ago, noted the "radical meaning" as "to touch," and then summarized the lexical evidence in terms of five meanings as applied in Greek literature beginning in the classical period and evolving through the centuries: (1) to pluck the hair; (2) to twang the bowstring; (3) to twitch the carpenter's line; (4) to touch the chords of a musical instrument, that is, to make instrumental music; (5) to touch the chords of the human heart, that is, to sing, to celebrate with hymns of praise (1911, p. 16; cf. Delling, 1972, 8:490). He then concluded that concerning the first four meanings, *psallo*

> had entirely lost all of these meanings before the beginning of the New Testament period, and that, therefore, the word is never used in the New Testament nor in contemporaneous literature in any of these senses. At this time, it not only meant to sing, but that is the only sense in which it was used, all the other meanings having entirely disappeared (pp. 44-45).

Psallo and English Translations

But what about the English translations? Do the **hundreds** of scholars responsible for translating the Greek New Testament into English support Rick's contention that *psallo* in Ephesians 5:19 refers to the use of instrumental music? Examine Appendix B, and you will see, once again, that the language scholars simply do not support Rick's claims. In fact, of the ten prominent translations consulted at each of the five occurrences of the word *psallo* in the Greek New Testament, **none** translate *psallo* "play," "play an instrument," or "make instrumental music." Specifically in Ephesians 5:19, the major translations have "making melody" (KJV, NKJV, ASV, NASB, ESV, RSV), "make music" (NIV, NEB), "sing with praise" (TEV), and "chanting"

(Jerusalem)—not one indication of mechanical instrumental music [NOTE: "music" is a generic term, like "melody," and does not in itself signify either vocal or instrumental music (*American Heritage...*, 2000, p. 1159). Contextual factors are necessary to ascertain what type of music is intended.] This circumstance is all the more remarkable in view of the fact that most, if not all, of the translators belong to denominations that use instrumental music in worship! In Curtis Vaughan's *The New Testament from 26 Translations*, only four English translations differ significantly from the KJV's rendering of "making melody" (1967, p. 888):

"Singing and **striking the strings** with your heart unto the Lord"—*Emphasized New Testament* (Rotherham)

"and **make melody** with the music of your hearts, to the Lord"—*The Epistles of Paul* (W.J. Conybeare)

"Sing and **make music** in your hearts"—*The Twentieth Century New Testament*

"and with your hearts sing and **play music** to the Lord"—*The N.T. in the Language of Today* (W.F. Beck)

Observe that the first three renderings pinpoint the heart as the place where the action of *psallo* occurs. Out of more than two dozen English translations, the closest any one comes to alluding to instrumental music is Beck's rendering "play music to the Lord." Yet, all these English translations (including Beck) render *psallo* in its other four occurrences in the New Testament as **singing**. **One** reference to **one** occurrence of *psallo* in a translation written by **one** man is flimsy justification for instrumental music. Question: If Rick's contention that "the bulk of scholarship disagrees" with the stance taken by churches of Christ, why haven't the translators included "to play an instrument" in their renderings of *psallo*?

Greek Theological Dictionaries and Commentaries

What about those specialists who are recognized as comprising the current Greek scholarship of the world in their production of the top Greek dictionaries and commentaries? Gerhard Delling wrote one of the pertinent articles in Kittel's prestigious *Theological Dictionary of the New Testament* (1972, 8:489-503). In his discussion of the word group that includes both *psallo* and *psalmos*, he notes that *psallo* occurs 40 times in the Septuagint for *zamar* in the Piel, sometimes meaning "to play a stringed instrument" unaccompanied by a song, and sometimes where singing and playing go together. He concludes: "Hence one must take into account **a shift of meaning in the LXX** [Septuagint—DM] in other passages in which **the idea of playing is not evident**" (8:494, emp. added). Not only have those who oppose the instrument been correct in their assertion that *psallo* had changed meaning by the time of the New Testament, this renowned Greek scholar insists that *psallo* had a shift in meaning **within the Greek Old Testament itself**! But that's not all that Delling has to say about *psallo*. He, in fact, affirms the very point that Rick denies regarding the transformation of *psallo* by New Testament times: "The expression *adontes kai psallontes* ["singing and making melody"— DM] in v. 19b underscores v. 19a. The combination of verbs in this order is found in the OT.... The literal sense 'by or with the playing of strings,' still found in the LXX [Septuagint— DM], is **now employed figuratively**" (8:498-499, emp. added). Delling insists that *psallo* in Ephesians 5:19 does not refer to literal playing on a physical instrument; rather, *psallo* is used figuratively! As if to anticipate those who argue that the references to instruments in heaven in the book of Revelation authorize instruments in Christian worship on Earth, he further observes: "The ref[erence] to stringed instruments in heavenly worship at Rev. 5:8; 15:2...**need not mean** that such instruments might sometimes accompany the singing at primitive Chr[istian] worship" (8:499, note 74, emp. added).

Another article in the *Theological Dictionary of the New Testament* was written by Heinrich Schlier on the Greek verb *ado*, which means "to sing." The participial form, found in Ephesians 5:19, is translated "singing." Schlier explains: "As 'to sing,' *adein* [to sing—DM] approximates to *humnesai, psallein* and *ainein* [to hymn, to make melody, and to praise—DM]. Indeed, **it can be used interchangeably with these terms.... There is no distinction from *psallein* in Eph. 5:19**" (1:164, emp. added). Schlier claims that the usual word for "singing" in the Greek is essentially a synonym for *psallo*—neither of which include within them an instrument.

In his article on *psalmos* in Colin Brown's *The New International Dictionary of New Testament Theology*, K.H. Bartels defines *psalmos* "a sacred song, psalm," and *psallo* "sing (a hymn or praise)" (1978, 3:670). After noting the secular, classical, and Old Testament meanings (pluck hair, twang a bow-string, then pluck a stringed instrument, then sing accompanied by musical instruments, then sing with or without accompaniment), Bartels notes two basic meanings in the New Testament for *psalmos*—(1) the Psalms of the Old Testament and (2) "a hymn of praise" (3:671). He then defines *psallo* in the New Testament as simply "to sing a spiritual or sacred song" (3:671). He pinpoints this meaning for all five occurrences of *psallo* in the New Testament, including Ephesians 5:19.

In his widely-acclaimed Greek Testament commentaries, first published in 1853, John Eadie comments on the use of *psallo* in Ephesians 5:19: "*Psallein*, originally 'to strike the lyre,' came to signify 'to strike up a tune,' and it denotes the prime accompaniment of these songs, to wit, **the symphony of the soul**. This is indeed secret and **inaudible melody....** 'playing in your hearts'" (1883, p. 402, emp. added).

In his 1890 *Word Studies in the New Testament*, Marvin Vincent discusses Ephesians 5:19 in his remarks on the occurrence of *psallo* in 1 Corinthians 14:15, where he renders the term "I will sing" (3:269). He then notes: "Some think that the verb has here its original signification of singing with an instrument." After reviewing briefly its sense in the Septuagint as well as six of the patristic writers, he concludes forthrightly: "The verb is used here in the general sense of **singing praise**" (3:270, emp. added).

In the *Exegetical Dictionary of the New Testament*, edited by Horst Balz and Gerhard Schneider, *psallo* is defined as: "This vb., which occurs 5 times in the NT, actually means 'pluck/play a stringed instrument' or 'sing to the accompaniment of a harp.' **In the NT it always refers to a song of praise to God**" (1993, 3:495, emp. added). In the *Word Biblical Commentary*, Andrew Lincoln pinpoints the meaning of *psallo* in Ephesians 5:19—"Although its original meaning involved plucking a stringed instrument, *psallo* here means **to make music by singing** (cf. also 1 Cor 14:15; Jas 5:13), so that **there is no reference in this verse to instrumental accompaniment**" (1990, p. 346, emp. added).

Summary

Do some commentators claim that *psallo* in Ephesians 5:19 inherently includes mechanical instrumental music? Yes, a few so claim. In doing so, like Rick, they fly in the face of the etymological transformation verified by linguistic history, placing themselves in opposition to the vast majority of New Testament Greek lexicographers. One example is A.T. Robertson who inconsistently claims that the meaning of *psallo* in Ephesians 5:19 is "to sing with an accompaniment" (although he does not specify what accompaniment), while its meaning in 1 Corinthians 14:15 is "to sing without regard to an instrument" (1931, 4:183; cf. 1934, p. 874). Nevertheless, the reader has been provided with significant Greek lexical evidence and multiple English translations, as well as Greek dictionaries and commentaries, that constitute abundant proof that it is simply not true that "the bulk of scholarship" supports Rick's claim.

But here is the "kicker." Let us assume that the original meaning of *psallo*—to touch, pluck, twitch, or twang—is the meaning intended by the Holy Spirit in Ephesians 5:19. Since the object on which the action of touching, plucking, twitching, or twanging does not inhere in the word, one would have to rely on the context to determine which instrument Paul intended. Surely no one would argue that one could worship God acceptably by snapping a carpenter's chalk line in the assembly, or shooting an arrow by flicking a bow string, or plucking hair. As evidenced in the lexical sources, one can *psallo* on all of these objects—a chalk line, a bow string, or hair. Hence, assuming that the original, radical meaning of *psallo* was intended by the Holy Spirit in this passage, even then sanction for **mechanical** instrumental music in worship cannot be extracted from its use in Ephesians 5:19. Why? For the simple reason that the instrument/object on which the action of *psallo* is to be done is **explicitly stated in the passage**. It is **the human heart**—the mind of the worshipper. Since one cannot physically, literally touch, pluck, twitch, or play the mind, it is obvious that the Holy Spirit spoke **figuratively**. He was calling attention to the fact that while one engages the lips and vocal chords in order to **sing** (*adontes*), it is essential that the worshipper also engage/enact the heart and mind as well (*psallontes*). Comparing Ephesians 5:19 and Colossians 3:16 proves that this conclusion is precisely what the Holy Spirit intended to convey:

Ephesians 5:18-19							
Be filled	speaking to	one another	in psalms, hymns, spiritual songs	singing	making melody (psallo)	in your heart	to the Lord
Let dwell	teaching admonishing	one another	in psalms, hymns, spiritual songs	singing	with grace	in your heart	to the Lord
Colossians 3:16							

The reader will observe that the Bible is its own best interpreter. The corresponding elements of Ephesians 5:19 and Colossians 3:16 match up exactly with each other, with the use of *psallo* in Ephesians 5:19 paralleling "with grace" in Colossians 3:16. Hence, "making melody" and "with grace" both refer to what occurs **spiritually** on the **inside** of the worshipper while he or she is **physically singing** on the **outside**. As B.W. Johnson explained in 1889: "While the lips sing, the heart must join in the melody by an uplifting to God. Too much singing in the churches is only of the lips" (2:202). Nineteenth century Presbyterian commentator Albert Barnes adds: "The idea here is that of **singing in the heart**, or praising God from the heart. The psalms, and hymns, and songs were to be sung **so that the heart should be engaged**" (1847b, p. 106, emp. added). F.F. Bruce concurred: "in their hearts as well as with their tongues" (1984, p. 380).

Representing the best in current evangelical scholarship, *The Expositor's Bible Commentary* well summarizes the linguistic data and the proper application of that data to a correct understanding of *psallo* in Ephesians 5:19—

> The verb "to make music" is psallo, from which "psalm" is derived. It can mean playing a stringed instrument (literally, "to pluck") or singing praise to the accompaniment of a harp. **Here it describes the heart's inner melody that keeps in tune with audible praise or may be independent of any outward expression** (Wood, 1981, 11:73, emp. added).

The action of *psallo* takes place in the heart independent of the outward expression of singing.

Grammatical Parallels

A precise parallel may be drawn between *psallo* and many other Greek verbs. The word *baptidzo* means to dip, immerse (Arndt and Gingrich, 1957, p. 131). A person can be immersed in water (John 3:23), fire, i.e., hell (Matthew 3:11), persecution and suffering (Mark 10:38-39; Luke 12:49), or the Holy Spirit (Acts 1:5). Observe that water, fire, suffering, and the Holy Spirit do not inhere in the word *baptidzo*/immerse. Immersion is an **action** that may occur with reference to a variety of elements or substances. Observe further that being immersed in water or fire is a **literal** use of *baptidzo*, while being immersed in suffering or the Holy Spirit is a **figurative** use of *baptidzo*.

Another example may be seen in the Greek verb *ballo*, to throw. One can throw seed on the ground (Mark 4:26), dust into the air (Acts 22:23), a fishhook into the sea (Matthew 17:27), a person on a sickbed (Revelation 2:22), or even fear (1 John 4:18). Observe that seed, dust, fishhooks, sickbeds, and fear do not inhere in the word *ballo*/throw. Observe further that throwing seed, dust, and hooks are **literal** uses of *ballo*, while throwing a person on a bed of affliction or casting out fear are **figurative** uses.

A third example is seen in the Greek verb *luo*, to loose, untie. One can loosen a prisoner (Acts 22:30), a sandal (Acts 13:25), grave clothes (John 11:44), angels (Revelation 9:14), sin (Revelation 1:5), or Satan (Revelation 20:3). Observe that prisoners, sandals, grave clothes, angels, sin, and Satan do not inhere in the word *luo*/loose. Observe further that loosing prisoners, sandals, or grave clothes are **literal** uses of *luo*, while loosing angels, sin, and Satan are **figurative** uses.

A fourth example is the Greek verb *phero*, to bear, carry, bring. One can carry, bear, or bring a cross (Luke 23:26), spices (Luke 24:1), an animal (Mark 11:2), food to eat (John 4:33), disgrace (Hebrews 13:13), or people's problems (Numbers 11:14). Observe that crosses, spices, animals, food, disgrace, and problems do not inhere in the word *phero*/bear. Observe further that bringing a cross, spices, an animal, or food are **literal** uses of *phero*, while bringing disgrace or bearing people's problems are **figurative** uses.

Many other examples could be cited. Please do not miss the point: the initial, literal meaning of *psallo*, to touch, pluck, etc., does not include or even imply the object on which the plucking takes place. Objects have included bow strings, carpenter lines, hair, lyres, etc. The specific object must be indicated in the context. To pluck on a mechanical instrument would be one possible **literal** use of *psallo*, whereas to pluck on the human heart is a **figurative** use of *psallo*—which happens to be the precise usage in Ephesians 5:19.

Quibble

In an effort to evade the conclusion that the heart is the instrument with/on which the *psallo*ing is to be done, a few have maintained that "in your heart" is used adverbially to mean "heartily," and so refers to **the manner** with which a **mechanical** instrument is to be played. However, most Greek scholars do not support this understanding of the underlying syntax. In the relevant phrase in Ephesians 5:19, *te kardia humon* (meaning "in the heart of you," i.e., "in your heart"), *te kardia* ("the heart") is in the Greek dative case. The term that describes this syntactical use has been identified as the "instrumental dative" or "dative of means" (see Dana and Mantey, 1927, pp. 88-91; Machen, 1923, pp. 60-61; Blass and Debrunner, 1961, pp. 104-105; Robertson, 1934, pp. 525ff.; Kuhner, 1853, pp. 417ff.).

In commenting on the relevant phrase, S.D.F. Salmond noted that

> the speaking one to another in psalms and hymns and spiritual songs was not to be a formal thing or a matter of the lips only, but **the utterance of the heart, "with** the heart" (RV).... Hence, it is best...to understand the clause as referring to **the melody that takes place in the stillness of the heart**. It specifies a second kind of praise in addition to that of the **lalountes**

[speaking—DM]—the **unvoiced** praise of **meditation and inward worship** (n.d., 3:364, emp. added).

Translating the phrase as "playing in your hearts," Eadie explains:

> The phrase, as Harless says, **does not mean heartily,** or *ek kardias* [literally "out of hearts"—DM] would have been employed. Compare Rom. i. 9—*en to pneumatic mou* ["in my spirit"—DM]. Theodoret comes nearer our view when he says—"He sings with his heart who not only moves his tongue, but also excites his mind to the understanding of the sentiments repeated".... Now this **silent playing in the heart** will be that sincere and genuine emotion, which ought to accompany sacred song. **The heart** pulsates in unison with the melody (1883, pp. 402-403, emp. added).

The great British scholar of the 19th century, J.B. Lightfoot, made the following comments on Colossians 3:16—

> This external manifestation must be accompanied by the inward emotion. There must be the thanksgiving of the heart, as well as the lips; comp. Ephes. v. 19 *adontes kai psallontes te kardia* ["singing and making melody in the heart"—DM] (probably the correct reading), **where** te kardia "with **the heart" brings out the sense more distinctly** (1875, p. 292, emp. added, italics and parenthetical item in orig.).

Calling attention to the remark of German scholar Harless, Henry Alford remarked, *"en kardia* ["in heart"—DM] **cannot,** being joined with *humon* ["your"—DM], **represent the abstract** 'heartily'" (1856, 3:135, emp. added, italics in orig.). In other words, the presence of the possessive pronoun "your" makes a rendering of "heartily" nonsensical ("in your heartily"?). As Wallace observes, the dative of manner (or adverbial dative) typically employs an **abstract** noun (1996, p. 161). "Heart" in Ephesians 5:19 is a concrete noun referring to the mind. In light of these observations, English translations that capture the literal sense include the ASV and NASB which translate the phrase "with your heart."

Other instances of *te kardia* in the dative without the preposition *en* ("in") include "understand with their hearts" (Matthew 13:15; Isaiah 6:10 [LXX]; Acts 28:27), in which the heart is the instrument used to understand; "with the heart one believes" (Romans 10:10) in which the heart is the instrument with which one believes; "as he purposes in his heart" (2 Corinthians 9:7) in which the heart is the instrument used to purpose; and "They always go astray in their heart" (Hebrews 3:10; Psalm 95:10 [LXX]) in which the heart is the instrument by which they go astray. Observe that the heart does not inhere in the actions of "understand," "believe," "purpose," and "go astray." The heart is the object, avenue, means, agency, instrument in/by/with which those actions occur. In like fashion, the instrument does not inhere in the action of *psallo*.

Even the Septuagint, to which Rick appeals for his claim that *psallo* includes the instrument, uses grammatical construction that parallels Ephesians 5:19, demonstrating that the action of *psallo* is separate and distinct from the object on which the action is performed. Compare the following parallels—

Ephesians 5:19	**make melody/ music**	in your heart	to the Lord
Psalm 33:2	**play**	on a psaltery of ten strings	to him
Psalm 71:22	**I will sing psalms**	on the harp	to thee
Psalm 92:1-3	**sing praises**	on a psaltery of ten strings	to thy name
Psalm 98:5-6	**sing**	with a harp	to the Lord
Psalm 144:9	**I will play**	on a psaltery of ten strings	to thee
Psalm 147:7	**sings praises**	on the harp	to our God
Psalm 149:3	**let them sing praises**	with timbrel and psaltery	to him

The bold face words in each of the above verses represent the translation of *psallo* in the Septuagint. If a mechanical instrument is automatically included in *psallo*, then each verse would have the psalmist saying that one must play the instrument to the Lord with the instrument: "I will play the harp to thee with the harp"; "I will play on a psaltery to thee on a psaltery." Such statements are nonsensical. Further, observe that each column matches perfectly. "In your heart" links up with, and is parallel to, the mechanical instruments specified in each of the psalms. We are forced to conclude that in the New Testament **the instrument on which the Lord requires music to be made is the human heart**.

Who Must *Psallo*?

Having previously established that the grammar of Ephesians 5:19 and Colossians 3:16 demonstrates that Paul refers to action that is to take place in the worship assembly of the church, we must ask the pertinent question: **who** is to participate in the actions alluded to in these verses? As already noted, the reflexive pronouns used reciprocally in both verses ("one another") **require** that all the members assembled for worship are to participate in the actions **together** (cf. Kuhner, 1853, p. 455). The specified actions of the participles (which carry an imperative force) are: "speaking," "singing," "teaching," "admonishing," and "making melody" (*psallontes*). The very nature of congregational singing is such that all these actions occur at the same time; that is, when Christians sing psalms, hymns, and spiritual songs together, they are likewise speaking to, teaching, and admonishing each other. When you and I sing together, I am speaking to you while you are speaking to me; I am teaching you at the same time that you are teaching me; we both **mutually** admonish each other. We must do this **together**, i.e., we must **both** participate **as the actions are occurring**. That is the meaning of these verses.

Hence, the "making melody" (*psallontes*) must also take place at the same time as the actions of singing, speaking, teaching, and admonishing, and ***the making melody must be***

done by the same ones who are doing the singing, speaking, teaching, and admonishing. Who is to do the **singing** in the assembly according to these two passages? Answer: the entire congregation. Who is to do the **admonishing** in the assembly according to these two passages? Answer: the entire congregation. The **speaking**? Everyone. The **teaching**? Everyone. All right then, who is to **make melody**? The entire congregation! If a manmade, mechanical instrument is inherent in *psallo* in Ephesians 5:19, then the only way to comply with God's directive is for **every Christian in the assembly to play an instrument while also singing**. And every Christian would have to do so at **every** service, even as every Christian is obligated by God to partake of the Lord's Supper, pray, and sing at the Sunday worship assembly of the church. No grammatical, linguistic, or biblical justification exists for confining the playing of instruments of music to a group smaller than the entire assembled congregation. Though Richland Hills has introduced instrumental music into its Saturday evening service, based on Rick's contentions, they are violating Ephesians 5:19 by omitting it from their Sunday worship assemblies. What's more, for literally centuries all the churches that have refrained from using instrumental music in their worship (including Richland Hills until February 10, 2007) have been displeasing to God in their worship since they have failed to engage in the action prescribed by the use of the term *psallo*.

Summary of *Psallo*

Abundant linguistic evidence disputes the claim that *psallo* automatically includes a mechanical instrument. Both Christians and non-Christians in the first century would have been familiar with the array of meanings that were associated with the word, and they certainly would have understood that the instrument does not inhere in the word itself, since context must establish the intended instrument.

Please observe very carefully that Rick has set forth two arguments that inherently contradict each other. On the one hand, he insists that the singing of Ephesians 5:19 has nothing to do with congregational worship ("nowhere in the New Testament is congregational singing specifically authorized"). Yet he claims to have authority to introduce instrumental music into **congregational** worship from the same passage. So according to him, Ephesians 5:19 authorizes instrumental music in the assembly, but does not authorize congregational singing in the assembly. His dual contentions are self-contradictory.

Rick insists that our problem is that we are trying to make "sing" to mean "sing only." But that is simply not the case. We sing because the New Testament instructs us to do so—specifically in Ephesians 5:19 by the use of the word *adontes*. We make melody (*psallontes*) with our hearts because Ephesians 5:19 tells us to do that, too. The reason we omit mechanical instruments of music is because neither Ephesians 5:19 nor any other New Testament passage instructs us to use instruments. Rick's illustrations do not help his case:

1. "When Paul said to Timothy, 'Take a little wine for your stomach's sake,' does that mean wine **only**? Would Timothy sin if he took wine and water?" The reason why Timothy was permitted to drink other liquids besides wine is because he had divine permission to do so prior to Paul's directive. From childhood, Timothy had been drinking other liquids, including water, with God's approval. He was authorized to do so, even as we are authorized to do so, since God created our bodies with a need for liquid. In the very verse to which Rick alludes, permission to drink water is inherent: "No longer drink **only water**, but use a little wine for your stomach's sake" (1 Timothy 5:23).

2. "When James says, 'Is anyone sick? Let him call the elders so they can come and anoint him with oil and pray for him.'

75

Well, if you called someone besides the elders, if you called the elders and some deacons, if you called the elders and your parents, did you sin because you didn't call the elders **only**?" Again, one must take into account context and the teaching of God's Word on this overall subject. The fact is that God authorizes us in other passages to enlist additional sources of assistance when we are sick, including family members, fellow believers, and doctors (e.g., Matthew 25:36; Mark 2:17; John 11:1ff.; et al.). Since we have Scripture that authorizes calling for a physician (Mark 2:17), and we have Scripture that authorizes calling for the elders, the only way for the Bible to harmonize with itself is for us to conclude that God authorizes us to call both a physician and the elders.

In order for either of these two illustrations to support Rick's position, he must provide Scriptures where, in addition to singing, God has instructed us to play mechanical instruments of music in worship to Him. Rick is unable to do so—since none exist.

Early Church History

Rick next claims that the word *psallo* was used to mean "play an instrument" by Josephus in the first century, by Suetonius in the second century, and by Chrysostom and Gregory of Nyssa as late as the fourth century. Once again, Rick has misconstrued the historical evidence. With almost one voice, specialists in patristic history have verified the fact that "[t]he rejection of all musical instruments from Christian worship is consistent among the Fathers" (Weakland, 1967, 10:106). In their monumental *Cyclopedia of Biblical, Theological, and Ecclesiastical Literature*, McClintock and Strong note that though the Greeks and Jews used instruments in religion,

it is generally believed that **the primitive Christians failed to adopt the use of instrumental music in their religious worship**.... The general introduction of instrumental music can certainly not be assigned to a date **earlier than the 5th and 6th centuries**.... The first organ is believed to have been used in Church service in **the 13th century**" (1876, 6:759, emp. added).

The *Catholic Encyclopedia* insists: "For almost a thousand years Gregorian chant, **without any instrumental or harmonic addition**, was the **only** music used in connection with the liturgy" (Otten, 1911, 10:657, emp. added). Gietmann observed: "Although Josephus tells of the wonderful effects produced in the Temple by the use of instruments, the first Christians were of too spiritual a fibre [*sic*] to substitute lifeless instruments for or to use them to accompany the human voice" (10:651).

James McKinnon conducted a sweeping analysis of the religious writings of the early centuries of Christianity in his Ph.D. dissertation at Columbia University and concluded that instruments were not used in the early church, but were a late innovation (1965). Recognized as a scholar in early church history and the patristic writers with a specialty in Gregory of Nyssa, Everett Ferguson contends that "[t]he testimony of early church history is **clear and strong** that early Christians employed vocal music but **did not employ instrumental music in their assemblies**" (1987, p. 79, emp. added). After a thorough review of the early Christian literature (i.e., the first three centuries after the close of the first), including the usage of *psallo* and *psalmos* in early church literature, Ferguson's conclusion is forceful and definitive:

> The case is now complete; the witnesses have been called and questioned. Their testimony is unmistakable: **early Christians sang unaccompanied by instrumental music in their assemblies**.... The evidence of church history confirms the reading of the New Testament that is found among the noninstrumental churches of Christ. **The historical argument is quite strong against early Christian use of instrumental music in church** (1987, pp. 97-98, emp. added).

Indeed, the historical evidence that the church of the first-century, and the early centuries that followed, rejected instrumental music in their assemblies is "virtually universal, uniform, and unanimous" (p. 98). The very use of the term *a cappella* proves that the early church did not use instruments in worship. Defined as "without instrumental accompaniment" (*American Heritage...*, 2000, p. 9), the expression is Latin/Italian for "in the manner of the church/chapel"—meaning that the established practice of the church was initially non-instrumental. Rick places himself in direct conflict with this voluminous and decisive historical evidence.

II. The Law of Exclusion/Silence of Scripture Argument

Rick notes that those who oppose the use of instrumental music argue that anything not specifically authorized in Scripture is forbidden, and though instruments were acceptable to God in the Old Testament, they would have to be re-authorized in the New Testament in order for Christians to have the right to use them. He then adds:

> Now, you're probably thinking, "But anti-instrument advocates do a lot of things the New Testament does not specifically authorize." Yes, they do. Yes, **we** do. We always have. We always will. Here's what we do: through a convenient assortment of mental gymnastics, we find a way to allow whatever we like as an aid, and we forbid whatever we dislike as an unauthorized addition. It's a **deeply** flawed way to read the Bible. It is **inherently** inconsistent. And it's **inevitably** divisive, and I don't think there is a single reason for all of the splits and the divisions in the Restoration Movement more than this single reason.

This statement betrays a fundamental misunderstanding of the biblical principle of authority. The fact of the matter is that the principle of authority as taught in the Bible, when followed, brings unity—not division. The division that Richland Hills is creating over instrumental music is partially due to the failure

78

to apply the principle of authority properly. By rejecting this principle, Rick throws open the door to a host of humanly devised practices that will only propel the church into further confusion, division, and disobedience.

The truth is, the idea that an action (like instrumental music) that is not specifically forbidden is acceptable to God is a deeply flawed way to read the Bible, it is inherently inconsistent, and inevitably divisive. Indeed, beyond the other motives given in Scripture for why people fail to arrive at God's truth (cf. Warren, 1982, p. 122), the approach Rick advocates likely is more responsible than any other for the splits and divisions in Christendom in general, and in the church in particular. Churches have split over how many cups to use in the Lord's Supper, not because of the "silence argument," but because of a failure to apply properly the concepts involved. **The reader is asked to weigh carefully the following assessment of the biblical doctrine of authority.**

The Biblical Principle of Authority

Perhaps no other doctrine is emphasized so frequently in Scripture as the principle of authority. Yet, perhaps no other doctrine is so discounted, ignored, rejected, or misunderstood. Nevertheless, the Scriptures make clear that, from the beginning of human history, God has required people to structure their behavior based upon His will. We humans have no **right** to formulate our own ideas concerning religious truth. **We must have God's approval for everything we do.**

Who could successfully deny that current culture is characterized by disrespect for authority? The "do your own thing" mentality that has been so pervasive since the 1960s has led those of subsequent generations to view themselves as autonomous (self-governing), with no higher authority than themselves. Authority is seen to reside inherently within the individual. This circumstance is reminiscent of the dark ages of Jewish history (the period of the Judges) when "everyone did what was right in his own eyes" (Judges 21:25).

Colossians 3:17: "In the Name of"

If the Bible teaches anything, it teaches that all human beings are under obligation to submit to the authority of God and Christ. Paul articulates this extremely important principle in his letter to the Colossians: "And whatever you do in word or deed, do all in the name of the Lord Jesus" (3:17). What does the apostle mean by that statement? What is the meaning of the expression "**in the name of the Lord**"?

Luke corroborates Paul's statement by providing the answer. Shortly after the establishment of the church of Christ on Earth (Acts 2), the Jewish authorities were extremely upset that the apostles were spreading Christian concepts throughout Jerusalem. So, they hauled Peter and John into their assembly and demanded to know, "By what **power** or by what **name** have you done this?" (Acts 4:7, emp. added). The word "power" (*dunamei*) bears a close correlation to and relationship with the concept of **authority** (Perschbacher, 1990, p. 108), and is closely aligned with *exousia*—the usual word for authority (cf. Luke 4:36; Revelation 17:12-13). W.E. Vine lists both terms under "power" (1940, p. 196). "Authority" (*exousia*) refers to power, rule, authority, or jurisdiction (cf. Betz, 1976, 2:608)— "the power of authority, the right to exercise power" and "the right to act" (Vine, pp. 152,89,196). It includes the ideas of "absolute power" and "warrant" (Arndt and Gingrich, 1957, p. 277), as well as "the 'claim,' or 'right,' or 'control,' one has over anything" (Moulton and Milligan, 1930, p. 225).

These religious leaders were demanding to know by what authority the apostles were acting. Who was giving them the **right** to teach what they were teaching? What authoritative source **approved** or **sanctioned** their particular actions? Peter's answer was "by the name of Jesus Christ" (vs. 10). In other words, the apostles had not been advocating their **own** ideas. They simply were presenting what Jesus had previously **authorized** and commissioned (cf. Matthew 16:19; 18:18; 28:18-20). He placed closure on the incident by concluding: "Nor is there salvation in any other, for there is **no other name** under heaven given among men by which we must be saved" (vs. 12, emp. added). Salvation may be achieved only by the authority, approval, sanction, and requirements of Christ. No one else on the planet has any **right or authorization** to extend salvation to anyone.

"In the name of" frequently is used in Scripture as a parallel expression to "by what power/authority." Hans Bietenhard noted that the formula "in the name of Jesus" means "according to his will and instruction" (1976, 2:654). In Acts 4:7, therefore, "[n]ame and 'power'...are used parallel to one another" (2:654). Vine writes that "name" in Colossians 3:17 means "in recognition of the authority of" (1940, p. 100; cf. Perschbacher, p. 294). Moulton and Milligan write that "name" refers to "the authority of the person" and cite Philippians 2:9 and Hebrews 1:4 as further examples (1930, p. 451). Observe carefully: "Therefore God also has highly exalted Him and given Him the **name which is above every name**, that at **the name of Jesus** every knee should bow, of those in heaven, and of those on earth" (Philippians 2:9-10, emp. added; cf. Ephesians 1:21). This is precisely what Jesus claimed for Himself when He issued the "Great Commission" to the apostles: "All **authority** has been given to Me in heaven and on earth" (Matthew 28:18, emp. added). Paul's reference to the **name** of Jesus is a reference to the **authority and jurisdiction** of Christ. Jesus' name being above every name means that His authority transcends all other authority. As Findlay explains: "'The name of the Lord Jesus' is the expression of his **authority** as 'Lord'" (Spence and Exell, 1958, p. 155, emp. added). A.T. Robertson cites the use of *onoma* in Matthew 28:19 as another example where "name" "has the idea of 'the authority of'" (1934, p. 740).

After Moses presented God's demands to Pharaoh, he returned to the Lord and complained that Pharaoh's reaction was retaliatory: "For since I came to Pharaoh to speak **in Your name**, he has done evil to this people" (Exodus 5:23, emp. added). For Moses to speak **in God's name** meant to speak **only those things that God wanted said**. After healing the lame man, Peter explained to the people: "And **His name**...has made this man strong" (Acts 3:16, emp. added). He meant that it was Christ's authority and power that achieved the healing. Likewise, when Paul became annoyed at the condition of the demon possessed slave girl, he declared: "I command you **in the name** of Jesus Christ to come out of her" (Acts 16:18, emp. added). He, too, meant that he had Christ's backing and authorization to do such a thing.

So when Paul states that everyone is obligated to speak and act "in the name of the Lord Jesus" (Colossians 3:17), he indicates that all human conduct must be conformed to the directives of Jesus Christ. Everything a person says or does must have the prior approval and sanction of God. Writing in 1855 from Glasgow, Scotland, New Testament scholar John Eadie well summarized the thrust of Colossians 3:17: "It...strictly means—**by his authority**, or generally, in recognition of it. To speak in His name, or to act in His name, is to speak and act not to His honour, but **under His sanction** and with the conviction of **His approval**" (1884, 4:249, emp. added).

Old Testament Illustrations

This biblical principle has enormous implications. No human being has the **right** to introduce into religious practice an activity for which the Scriptures provide no approval. In God's sight, we human beings are simply not free to fashion religion and morality according to our own desires. Cain learned that the hard way when he failed to offer the precise sacrifice that God had designated (Genesis 4:5-7; Hebrews 11:4; 1 John 3:12). The lives of Nadab and Abihu were snuffed out by God because of what they must have viewed as a minor adjustment in their offering (Leviticus 10:1-2). They were the right boys, at the right time and place, with the right censers, and the right incense—but the wrong fire. This deviation from God's precise specifications is identified as "unauthorized" (NIV) fire "which He had not commanded them" (NKJV). The change failed to show God as **holy** and give Him the **respect** He deserves (Leviticus 10:3).

Saul was rejected by God when he presumed to offer a sacrifice he was not authorized to offer (1 Samuel 13:8-14). He was censured a second time for making slight adjustments in God's instructions (1 Samuel 15:22-23). Ultimately, he lost his crown and the approval of God. Justifying his adjustments on the grounds that he merely was attempting to be "culturally relevant" would not have altered his status in God's sight. Uzzah was struck dead simply because he touched the Ark of the Covenant, though his apparent motive was to **protect** it (2 Samuel 6:6-7). David admitted that the nation had deserved the Lord's displeasure because they were not seeking God "after the due order" (1 Chronicles 15:13; cf. Numbers 4:15; 7:9; 10:21). In other words, God had given previous information concerning proper or **authorized** transportation of the Ark, but these instructions were not followed. Their handling of the Ark was not done "in the name of the Lord," in that they did it **their** way instead of according to the divine prescription.

Notice that these cases involved **religious** people who were engaged in **religious** activities. They were not pagans, skeptics, or atheists. They were attempting to worship the **one true God.** They were **believers!** Yet their failure to conform precisely to divine instructions elicited the disapproval of God for the simple reason that their actions were **unauthorized**.

The New Testament illustrates this principle repeatedly. Authority begins with God. He delegated authority to Jesus (Matthew 28:18; John 5:27). Only Jesus, therefore, has the authority to define and designate the parameters of human behavior in general and religious practice in particular. Consequently, no human being on Earth has the right to do **anything** without the prior approval of Christ. John said that those who believe on Christ's **name** (i.e., those who accept His **authority**) have the **power or right** to become children of God. In other words, faith is a necessary prerequisite that gives a person divine **authority** to become a child of God. All other human beings, i.e., unbelievers, lack divine sanction to become children of God.

A Roman centurion, an officer who commanded one hundred men, understood the principle of authority. He said to Jesus: "For I also am a man under authority, having soldiers under me. And I say to this one, 'Go,' and he goes; and to another, 'Come,' and he comes; and to my servant, 'Do this,' and he does it" (Matthew 8:9). This centurion recognized that individuals who are subject to the authority of a higher power must receive **permission** for everything they do. They must conform themselves precisely to the will of their superior.

Even the religious enemies of Jesus understood and acknowledged the principle of authority. One day when Jesus was teaching in the temple, the chief priests and elders confronted Him with two questions: "By what authority are You doing these things? And who gave You this authority?" (Matthew 21:23). Commenting on the use of the term "authority," Betz notes that the Pharisees used the term *exousia* to refer to "the power to act which given as of right to anyone by virtue of the position he holds" (1976, 2:601). They were asking, in essence, "Who conferred upon you this authority which you presume to exercise? Was it some earthly ruler, or was it God himself?" (Spence and Exell, 1961, 15:321). Even these religiously warped opponents of our Lord at least grasped correctly the concept that **one must have prior approval from a legitimate authoritative source** before one can advocate religious viewpoints. As Williams noted: "No one could presume to teach without a proper commission: where was his authorization?" (quoted in Spence and Exell, 1961, 15:320). If Jesus agreed with the pro-instrumentalist viewpoint, He would have said, "What do you mean 'by what authority'? God doesn't require us to have authority for what we do in religion as long as we do not violate a direct command that forbids it, and as long as we are sincere."

But Jesus was not in sympathy with today's permissive, antinomian spirit. In fact, His response to the Jewish leaders showed that He agreed fully with the principle of authority (after all, He authored it). He proceeded to show them that His teaching was **authorized** by the same source that authorized the teaching of John the Baptizer. Yet, these hardhearted religious leaders rejected John and, by implication, his source of authority. So neither would they accept Jesus, Who received His authority from the same source (i.e., Heaven). In any case, both Jesus and His enemies agreed that **one must have God's prior permission** for what one advocates in religion.

What does Peter mean when he writes, "If anyone speaks, let him speak as the oracles of God" (1 Peter 4:11)? He means that whatever a person advocates in religion must be found in God's Word. But religious activities such as baby dedication services, handclapping, instrumental music, choirs, praise teams, the worship of Mary, non-Sunday observance of the Lord's Supper, and church raffles are not found in God's Word. Thus, their use violates the principle of authority—failing to "speak as the oracles of God."

What does Paul mean when he writes, "...that you may learn in us not to think beyond what is written" (1 Corinthians 4:6)? He means that whatever we do in religion first must be found in the Scriptures. But "sacred drama," swaying arms, and religious observance of Christmas and Easter are not found in Scripture. Their use violates the principle of authority—thinking and going "beyond what is written."

Illustrations from Secular Society

Interestingly enough, even secular society acknowledges the principle of authority. The average American citizen will walk into a restaurant and see two doors. The first door has the word "Restrooms" on it, while the second door has the words "Authorized Personnel." These messages are immediately interpreted to mean that the customer has authority to enter the door that reads "Restrooms," while he or she is not permitted to enter the other door. In fact, one instantly knows that no **authority** exists to enter the second door—even though the sign does not **explicitly** command the customer **not** to enter the door. The sign does not indicate who may **NOT** enter. It only specifies who **may** enter—who has **permission or authority** to enter. The customer is under obligation to use reasoning powers and to deduce that he or she has no authority to pass through the second door.

Entering the first door, the customer encounters two additional doors. The first door has a stick figure of a woman on it, while the second door has a stick figure of a man. Once again, the customer is expected to understand that only women are authorized to enter the first door, and only men have permission to pass through the second door—**though the word "only" does not appear**. People fathom the principle of authority so easily and so thoroughly that they can ascertain what they may or may not do even from pictures—stick figures! But when it comes to the Christian religion and those who wish to broaden the parameters of God's Word by introducing unauthorized worship practice, recognition of the principle of authority is set aside in exchange for irrational, emotional desire to do what one **wants** to do.

When we purchase a new vacuum cleaner or a new car, the product comes with a factory warranty which provides the customer with free repair service for the specified warranty period. However, should a malfunction occur, the customer is instructed to take the product to a "Factory-Authorized Representative." Failure to do so will void the warranty. Does the average person understand the principle of authority in this case? Of course we do. We understand that the manufacturer has given prior approval to a select group of repairpersons who are **authorized** to repair the product. We understand that we have **authority/permission** to take the product to any of those places, but that we are **not authorized** to take the product anywhere else—even though other repairpersons are not specifically singled out as unacceptable or forbidden.

When a person enters the hospital for surgery, he or she signs a document authorizing the physician to operate. What would you think of a doctor, whom you have authorized to perform surgery on you, if he were to go out into the waiting room where your family is awaiting your return and commence to operate on your child? In addition to thinking he may be mentally ill, you would protest his **lack of authority** for his action. What if he justified his action by insisting that **you did not specifically forbid** his performing surgery on your loved one? What if he said, "You did not state that I am to operate on you **only**." Neither you—nor the medical and legal professions—would put up with such nonsense. Why? Normal people understand and live by the principle of authority. But religion is different. Nonsense and abnormality seem to have become the order of the day.

What if your doctor wrote you a prescription for antibiotics, and you took it to the pharmacist, who then filled the prescription by giving you the antibiotic—laced with strychnine? On reading the label, you immediately would protest the pharmacist's action and demand an explanation. Would the pharmacist be considered in her right mind if she offered as her explanation, "The doctor did not say I was **not** to give you the poison. I interpreted his silence to be permissive"? What if she insisted, "The doctor's command neither prescribes nor prohibits strychnine"? Yet Rick insists that "New Testament commands to sing neither prescribe nor prohibit instrumental music." **Rick's statement is precisely parallel to: "The doctor's command to give antibiotic neither prescribes nor prohibits strychnine."**

Suppose you send a note to your child at school instructing him to stop by the grocery store on his way home from school and to purchase a gallon of 2% milk and a one-pound loaf of wheat bread. When he returns home, he has a gallon of 2% milk, a one pound loaf of **white** bread, and a box of Twinkies©. Do you pat him on the head and compliment him for his faithful obedience? Do you praise him for his effort, talent, and sincerity? Or do you challenge his behavior as being **unauthorized**? What if he justifies his actions by insisting that **you said nothing** about the purchase of white bread and Twinkies©? Concerning instrumental music, Rick declares: "You can't open your Bible and show me where God forbids it." So what if your child hands you the written note you sent to him and declares: "You can't open your note and show me where you forbade it." The fact is, both you and he would know that he engaged in unauthorized behavior. He did not have your **permission** to purchase white bread or Twinkies©—even though you did not specifically forbid it.

When you place an order at a drive-through window of a fast food restaurant, you expect them to conform to your instructions precisely, neither adding to nor subtracting from your order. Suppose at the speaker, you order a Big Mac©, large fry, and a large Diet Coke©. You then pull forward to the window and the cashier says, "That will be $435.87," as she and her co-workers begin handing bag after bag of food to you, bags that contain large quantities of every food item on the menu. You immediately would ask her to stop, and you would insist that you did not order all that food. What would you think if she responded: "You did not order a Big Mac©, large fry, and large Diet Coke© **only**. You did not **forbid** us to give you additional food." You would think this person is either joking—or crazy. The restaurant workers receive authority from you based on **what you say** to them—not based on what you do **not** say. You do not give them authority for their actions on the basis of your **silence**. You authorize them by your **words**, your instructions, your directions. If they go beyond the parameters of your words—though you do not specifically forbid such actions—they are proceeding **without your authority**. So it is with our relationship with God and His Word (cf. Deuteronomy 4:2; 5:32; 12:32; Joshua 1:7; Proverbs 30:6). God instructed us to worship Him by singing. He did not instruct us to worship Him by playing. Hence, to worship with instruments is to worship God without His approval.

Authority For EVERYTHING?

But does that mean that we must have authority for **everything** we do in religion? **Everything**? What about the many things we do that the Bible does not mention? For example, where is our authority for church buildings, pews, lighting, carpet, television programs, songbooks, and communion trays?

Consider the case of Noah. He was instructed by God to construct a large wooden boat. That meant he was not authorized to build some other type of vessel. God's instructions included such details as dimensions, type of wood, a door and window, and decks (Genesis 6:14-16). The principle of authority applied to Noah in the following fashion (see chart):

HOW THE BIBLE AUTHORIZES 1					
If God Said	**Build a Vessel**				
Types of Vessels	Car	Plane	**Boat**	Motorcycle	Train
Types of Materials	Plastic	Fiberglass	**Wood**	Plexiglas©	Metal
Types of Wood	Pine	Cedar	**Gopher**	Oak	Poplar

He was authorized to build a boat, but not authorized to build an alternative mode of transportation (e.g., car, plane, or balloon). He was authorized to make the boat out of wood, but not authorized to make it out of some other material (e.g., plastic, steel, or fiberglass). He was authorized to use "gopherwood," but not authorized to use some other kind of wood (e.g., oak, poplar, or pine).

Noah had authority from God to build a gopherwood boat. He would have been guilty of sin if he had built a pinewood boat or a Plexiglas© airplane—not because God forbade him to do it, and not because God said, "Build a gopherwood boat **only**"—but because he would have lacked God's permission/authority to do so.

Observe further that Noah was authorized to utilize whatever tools and assistance were necessary to comply with God's command (e.g., hammers, nails, saws, hired help). Though nails and hammers were not specifically mentioned by God, they were fully **authorized** by Him since they were inherently necessary in order to comply with God's directive to build a boat. Instruments, on the other hand, do **not** enable a person to obey the command to sing. They supplement singing with an alternative form of making music. They no more aid the command to sing than hamburgers aid the command to eat the Lord's Supper:

HOW THE BIBLE AUTHORIZES 2			
Command:	**Eat Lord's Supper**	**Sing**	**Build Boat**
Aids	Cups Trays Attendants	Pitch pipe Song Leader Song Books	Hammers Nails Workers
Additions	Coke Hamburgers	Organ Piano	Oak Poplar

Consider the Great Commission. God commanded His emissaries to "Go" (Mark 16:15). The Bible tells of various inspired preachers who **went** by using many different acceptable means, including by chariot (Acts 8:31), by rope and basket (Acts 9:25), on foot (Acts 14:14), and by ship (Acts 16:11). Gathering together everything in the Scriptures pertaining to this matter, it becomes clear that the mode of transporting the Gospel is **optional**. Therefore, the Bible interpreter is forced to conclude that every mode is **authorized** today (including, for example, television), as long as it does not violate some other biblical principle (e.g., the principle of stewardship).

This process of gathering biblical evidence and drawing only warranted conclusions is divinely mandatory for every human being (see 1 Thessalonians 5:21; 1 John 4:1). We are under obligation to weigh the biblical data on every subject and conclude only what God wants us to conclude. [For concise, definitive analyses of the principle of authority, see Warren, 1975; Warren, 1986; Deaver, 1987].

The Bible enjoins upon us the act of assembling together for worship (e.g., Acts 20:7; 1 Corinthians 5:4; 11:17-18; Hebrews 10:25). It is physically impossible for a plurality of individuals to assemble together without an assembly place—they must assemble **somewhere**. We have approved instances of the early church assembling together in a third-story room (Acts 20:8-

9), in private residences, as well as in non-private settings (1 Corinthians 16:19; 11:22; cf. Acts 20:20). We are forced to conclude that the location is **optional and authorized**, as long as it does not violate other biblical principles (cf. John 4:21). Hence, the Scriptures **authorize** church buildings and the necessary furnishings (e.g., carpet, chairs, lights [see Acts 20:8], restrooms, drinking fountains).

The same may be said of songbooks. Christians are commanded to sing (Ephesians 5:19; Colossians 3:16) and to worship in an orderly manner (1 Corinthians 14:40). God wants us to sing the same song together (as opposed to singing different songs at the same time—cf. 1 Corinthians 14:26-33). Ways to comply with these stipulations would be to use songbooks, sheet music, or projectors that give the entire assembly access to the same song at the same time. Therefore, all such tools are **authorized as expedient ways** to comply with the command to sing.

Instrumental music in worship is not authorized. While some people may think it qualifies as an expedient—an aid to their singing—it does not. It may drown out their singing, or so overshadow it that they **think** it sounds better, but in actuality a musical instrument merely **supplements** singing. It is **another form of music** in the same way that seeing and hearing are two distinct ways of perceiving. Seeing does not aid hearing; it supplements one form of perception/observation with another. Consider the following chart:

HOW THE BIBLE AUTHORIZES 3					
Command:	Travel		Perceive		Make Music	
How to Obey	Walk	Ride	See	Hear	Sing	Play
Aids/ Expedients	Cane Shoes	Car Horse Bicycle	Glasses Contacts	Hearing Aid	Pitch pipe Songbook Leader	Piano Organ
Additions	Car Horse Bicycle	Cane Shoes	Nose	Glasses Binoculars	Piano Organ	Singing Voice Lessons

Singing with the voice and **playing** on a mechanical instrument are two separate ways of **making music**. Singing is authorized because the New Testament enjoins it (Ephesians 5:19; Colossians 3:16). God has told us He wants us to sing. Instrumental music is unauthorized—not because Ephesians and Colossians exclude it or don't mention it—but because **no New Testament passage enjoins it**. Nowhere does God inform us that He desires that we play on an instrument to Him. To do so is to "add to His words" (Proverbs 30:6) and to "go beyond what is written" (1 Corinthians 4:6).

The Lord's Supper is to be eaten when the church is assembled for worship (Matthew 26:29; Acts 20:7; 1 Corinthians 11:20). God wants each worshipper to partake of both the bread and the grape juice. How may this be accomplished? Containers or trays are necessarily required—unless grapes are hand carried to each person who would then squeeze the juice into his or her own mouth. We have the account of Jesus instituting the Lord's Supper and apparently using a single cup. However, the context makes clear that the container was incidental—representing a figure of speech known as "metonymy of the subject," in which the container is put for the contained (Dungan, 1888, p. 279). The **content** of the cup—the juice—was what they were to drink, and upon which they were to reflect symbolically. We are forced to conclude that the manner of distribution of the elements of the Lord's Supper is **authorized** as optional.

Summary

Every single facet of our behavior, in and out of worship, may be determined in the same way. God so requires. He expects us to give heed to His Word, studying it carefully and consistently in order to know how to live life in harmony with His will. For true Christianity to be practiced, we must be true to God's directions. We must be faithful to the book. Indeed, for Jesus to be the "Lord of my life" 24-7, I must ascertain **His** will in every decision of my life. Hezekiah "did what was good and right and true before the Lord his God" (2 Chronicles 31:20). To what do the words "good," "right," and "true" refer? The next verse explains: "And in every work that he began in the service of the house of God, in the law and in the commandment, to seek his God, he did it with all his heart" (2 Chronicles 31:32). Hezekiah was faithful to God, doing what was good, right, and true—in the sense that **he obeyed precisely the law and commandments of God**, and did so from the heart (cf. John 4:24).

Many churches that claim to be Christian have introduced into their belief and practice all sorts of activities, programs, and practices that have no basis in Scripture—i.e., no indication from God that He approves. Upon what basis are these innovations justified? "Well, it meets our needs"; "It gets more people involved"; "It brings in lots of people"; "It generates enthusiasm"; "It allows us to get things done"; "We really like it"; "It stimulates interest"; "It keeps our young people's attention"; "It creates a warm, accepting environment"; "It is a good mission strategy." It is absolutely incredible that so many Christians could drift so far from biblical moorings. Their failure to recognize the principle of Bible authority will not exempt them from God's disfavor.

When all is said and done, and we've rationalized doing whatever we wish in worship, we are still faced with this need: our actions must be in accordance with God's instructions. By definition, being **faithful** to God entails conformity to divine directives—right doing (1 John 3:7; Acts 10:35). When one "transgresses (i.e., goes ahead), and does not abide in the doctrine of Christ" (2 John 9), he becomes **unfaithful** and removes himself from the benefits of God's grace (2 Peter 2:20-22; Hebrews 10:26-31; Galatians 5:4). Remaining within the grace and favor of God depends on our compliance with the all-important, God-ordained principle of authority.

Must we conform ourselves to **the name** of Christ? That is, in order to be saved, must I have His prior approval, His sanction, His authorization, His permission for everything I do in religion? Peter answers: "Nor is there salvation in any other, for there is **no other name** under heaven given among men by which we must be saved" (Acts 4:12).

Jesus, the Synagogue, & the Feast of Lights

Rick attempts to bolster his rejection of the authority principle with the following claims:

> And by the way, one more thought: if it is a sin to worship God except as He has specifically told you to do, then Jesus violated the law of silence. Where, anywhere, in the Bible does God authorize the synagogue? No where. Jesus went to synagogues. Where, anywhere in the Bible, does God authorize a "Feast of Lights"? That was started by the Maccabees in the intertestamental period. But in John chapter 10, Jesus went to the Feast of Lights.

These claims are characterized by completely unwarranted assumptions. Consider two reasons why Rick's claim concerning synagogues does not prove his point:

1. Though the Law of Moses dictated that certain religious observances especially connected to Levitical/priestly activity were to be conducted at the central worship site (the temple) in Jerusalem, the people were authorized to engage in additional religious activity in their private lives and respective locations. Would Rick claim that praying to God could take place only in Jerusalem? The fact is that a Jew could pray to God anytime, anywhere. He obviously would have prayed to God while surrounded by his family in his own home. Daniel, who was meticulous about obeying the Law, prayed three times a day while in Babylon (Daniel 6:10). If several Jews could pray and read the Old Testament together in a private home apart from Jerusalem, it would follow that the Jews next door could

participate with them. Suppose that several families on the same street decided to meet together for that purpose, but none of their homes was large enough to accommodate the number. Would they be authorized by God to build a separate building for those who desired to pray together and read the Old Testament aloud? Of course. Logically, then, synagogues would be authorized (cf. Psalm 74:8). However, the parameters of such worship would be biblically limited, omitting those activities that God directed to be performed only in Jerusalem and only by qualified individuals (i.e., priests and Levites).

2. Let's suppose, however, that synagogues were unauthorized by God. Rick makes another unwarranted assumption when he insists that by Jesus entering a synagogue, He was violating the law of silence. He is assuming that Jesus could not enter a synagogue without being guilty of implying approval of the synagogue. But that is a false assumption. I visited a Hindu temple in Dallas some years ago. I observed worshippers clinking their miniature hand cymbals, strumming instruments, and even lying face down on the floor—all directed to the wooden deity situated at the front of the room. I have also visited other religious assemblies that included worship actions that are unauthorized by God. Suppose I was invited to speak at one such gathering and allowed to say whatever I desired concerning God's Word. Would my acceptance of such an invitation automatically implicate me as guilty of endorsing that religion or approving of the gathering? Of course not. So why make such an assumption about the Son of God when He visited synagogues? One would have to have some indication from the context that He participated in such a way as to inherently endorse synagogue worship. His presence may only indicate His desire to locate a ready audience to whom to present God's will. Is there any textual indication as to the **purpose** of Jesus visiting synagogues? Absolutely: He used them as opportunities to teach people God's Word, confronting the corruptions of

authorized religion and demonstrating His deity by performing miracles: "Jesus replied, 'Let us go somewhere else—to the nearby villages—**so I can preach there also**. That is why I have come.' So he traveled throughout Galilee, **preaching in their synagogues** and driving out demons (Mark 1:38-39, emp. added; cf. 3:1-2; Luke 4:15-16,31ff.; Also see McGarvey, n.d., pp. 174-175).

Rick makes an even greater leap when he implies that by being present in the temple during the Feast of Lights, Jesus approved of unauthorized religious worship. He cites John 10. A simple reading of that passage refutes Rick's claim: "Then came the Feast of Dedication at Jerusalem. It was winter, and Jesus was in the temple area walking in Solomon's Colonnade. The Jews gathered around him, saying, 'How long will you keep us in suspense? If you are the Christ, tell us plainly'" (John 10:22-24—NIV). Observe that the text does not state, as Rick implies, that "Jesus went to the Feast of Dedication to participate in the festivities/worship." The text simply says that during the Feast of Dedication, Jesus was walking in the temple area—specifically Solomon's Colonnade. As previously noted, this area had nothing to do with Jewish worship. It was a spacious, convenient location in which to interact with others. As Jesus was milling around, certain Jews pressed in around Him—just the situation that Jesus sought to elicit. Having affirmed His deity to them, and to those who must have witnessed the interchange, they picked up stones to stone Him (vs. 31—further proof that "temple" is a loose expression, since stones were lying around), and then attempted to seize Him, but He "escaped their grasp" (vs. 39) and left town, crossing back over the Jordan River (vs. 40). Apparently, Jesus was less interested in actually participating in the Feast of Lights than Rick suggests. Other passages show that Jesus' purpose and presence was not to endorse Hanukkah, but to teach (Luke 19:47; 20:1; 21:37-38; John 7:14,28; 8:2,20; 10:22ff.; 18:20).

By Rick's "reasoning," since Jesus also interacted with the Sadducees (e.g., Matthew 22:23ff.), He endorsed their brand of Judaism, their concocted sect, and their doctrines—which included a denial of the resurrection (Matthew 22:23ff.). And that would mean that Paul approved of paganism and Greek/ Roman mythology, since he visited Mars Hill in Athens and attended "the meeting of the Areopagus" (Acts 17:22—NIV), intermingling with pagan philosophers. To show the fallacy of this line of thinking: Would Rick claim that God authorizes synagogue worship **today**? Surely not, since Judaism has been discarded, and Jewish worship is no longer acceptable to God. Yet Paul attended the synagogue **after** Christianity was established, engaging in logical disputation with attendees (Acts 17:1ff.). Hence, we conclude that Jesus' presence in synagogues does not prove that Jesus violated the "law of silence," nor that today one may engage in practices as long as they are not specifically forbidden by God.

Wine at Passover

Rick attempts to support his view by asking, "Where in the Bible does the Passover meal authorize using cups of wine? No, you go read it. You go read what God authorized in the Passover. He doesn't mention wine one time." He then concludes that if you can add wine to the Passover meal, you can add instruments to singing. Once again, Rick has obscured the true issue. God gave no legislation regarding the consumption of liquids at the Passover meal, but confined His directives to the food— roasted lamb, bitter herbs, and unleavened bread (Exodus 12:8-9; Numbers 9:11). Consequently, the Israelites were free to exercise their own discretion regarding any drink that accompanied the food—since they already were authorized to consume liquids (as we are) by divine design (e.g., Deuteronomy 32:14; 1 Kings 17:4; 1 Corinthians 9:4,7; Colossians 2:16).

Observe that food and drink are not parallel to each other as are singing and playing instruments. A correct parallel lies in whether the Israelites were authorized by God to add any other types of **food** to the meal. Would God have been pleased if, in addition to roast lamb, the Israelites added roast duck, baked turkey, or fried chicken? Were they authorized to include yeast donuts in addition to unleavened bread? The answer to these questions is obvious. Singing is to playing what lamb is to turkey. Singing and playing are species of music. Lamb and turkey are species of food. Singing and playing are not parallel to eating food and drinking wine.

Command:	Eat the Passover	Eat the Lord's Supper	Sing
Aids	Fire Plates	Cups Trays	Songbooks
Additions	Duck Turkey	Lemonade Hamburgers	Guitar Drums

Rick's summary declaration is: "The point simply is this: Jesus did not allow His worship of God to be restricted by the very law that we've tried to bind on our brothers and sisters." But as shown above, the proofs for this conclusion are no proof at all. Throughout Bible history, God restricted worship by expecting people to conform themselves to His instructions without addition or subtraction (Deuteronomy 4:2; Proverbs 30:6). The Bible is permeated by numerous instances of the principle of "silence," and only those who refrain from studying their Bibles will be influenced by Rick's sweeping generalizations and mischaracterizations.

God "Saying Nothing"?

Rick continues: "I want to ask you this question: What great message of God did He ever communicate by saying nothing about it?" In so stating, two critical realities are conveniently ignored: (1) God **did** say something about acceptable worship—

explicitly, forthrightly, and directly. He said, "Sing to Me" (Ephesians 5:19; Colossians 3:16; et al.). He did not say, "Play to Me." (2) And remember that God frequently communicated central doctrines without specifically denouncing or forbidding various related aspects. For example, the New Testament communicates the great principle of respecting our bodies (e.g., 1 Corinthians 6:12-20). But He said **nothing** about ingesting marijuana, LSD, or crack cocaine. Rick's contention implies that since God failed to communicate specifically about refraining from illegal drug use, we may use them. Further, you can read your Bible from cover to cover and you will not find any communication from God forbidding our having a Pope over Christ's church, or condemning entrance into Islam, Buddhism, or Hinduism. Using Rick's rationale, these approaches are acceptable to God. The unrealistic expectations he places on God's Word are concocted, contrived, and unbiblical.

Imagine how long the Bible would have to be if God had to forbid specifically every action He did not approve. "[T]he world itself could not contain the books that would be written" (John 21:25). Imagine if God had to specifically forbid every food and liquid that He does not want used in the Lord's Supper. Imagine if He had to explicitly prohibit every worship action conjured up by humans over the millennia. Imagine if He had to specifically forbid or denounce every manmade religion invented in human history. Imagine if He had to specifically exclude every liquid except water for baptism. Such an approach to the Bible places an irrational, and frankly asinine, expectation on God—an expectation that no human places on himself.

As if to anticipate Rick's twisted treatment of Scripture, the Holy Spirit used precisely the same reasoning that Rick rejects. In establishing the high priesthood of Jesus in our behalf, the writer of Hebrews had to demonstrate that Jesus' priesthood was not according to the Law of Moses (since no ultimate forgiveness was available under that system). Instead, Jesus' priesthood is parallel to the pre-Mosaic priesthood of Melchizedek. Jesus could not have been a priest under the Law of Moses since those priests were from the tribe of Levi, and Jesus was from the tribe of Judah. The writer explains: "He of whom these things are said belonged to a different tribe, and no one from that tribe has ever served at the altar. For it is clear that our Lord descended from Judah, and in regard to that tribe Moses **said nothing** about priests" (Hebrews 7:13-14). Incredible! By the power of the Holy Spirit, the Hebrews writer argued that the Law of Moses did not authorize priests from any tribe but Levi—not because it was specifically **forbidden**—but because **the Law said nothing about it.** If Rick had lived in the first century and had the opportunity to give his input, he would have accused the inspired writer of using "a **deeply** flawed way to read the Bible," one that is "inherently inconsistent," and "inevitably divisive." Yet, here is a great message from God (the high priesthood of Jesus), one aspect of which He communicated by saying **nothing** about it, in direct contradiction to Rick's claim.

Rick then added:

> You parents think about this for a second. If you punished your children for what you call disobedience, over something you never talked about, are you a good father, a good mother? If you get rebellious children, you get what you deserve. The Father in heaven makes it clear what He expects of us. And He does not communicate to us by saying nothing.

Rick, yet again, obscures and sidesteps the key issue. He acts as if God "never talked about" how He expects to be worshipped—when He has, in fact, spoken **definitively.** Rick unwittingly admits this fact when he declared: "The Father in heaven makes it clear what He expects of us." Indeed, He explicitly told us to "sing." Rick's illustration regarding good parents is completely irrelevant. A more applicable illustration is the one given earlier:

a parent gives a child instructions and the child presumes to **add** to those directives on the grounds that the parent did not specifically forbid the child to make those additions. If a doctor instructs a pharmacist to give his patient antibiotic, and the pharmacist gives the patient antibiotic and arsenic—on the grounds that the doctor "never talked about" the arsenic—to be consistent, Rick would need to label the pharmacist a "good pharmacist" and chide the doctor for inciting rebellion in the pharmacist who merely exercised her "gift."

"What It Says About the Bible"

Rick proceeds to pinpoint two problems he has with the anti-instrumental viewpoint. The first has to do with what it says about the Bible.

> I've always resonated with the idea that a simple and sincere student of Scripture could read and understand God's will. Now I still do. That's why I must reject the anti-instrument position. No one not already indoctrinated would arrive at such a conclusion without someone teaching them to read the text through their particular interpretive grid. Let me say that again. Nobody who just sincerely read the Bible for the first time would ever reach the conclusion that instrumental praise was unacceptable to God, unless you came after they had read the Bible and taught them to read the Bible your way.

This point has already been refuted. But observe very carefully again just how judgmental, presumptuous, and unkind this claim is since many people have come honestly and sincerely to the very conclusion Rick rejects. The fact of the matter is that if you were to sit down and read the New Testament from Matthew to Revelation with a view toward understanding how God would have a Christian to worship Him, one would never get the idea that God desired use of instrumental praise, since He never so indicates that desire. On the other hand, one would **clearly and unmistakably** conclude that God desires that worshippers **sing**. Simply read every verse in the New

Testament that says anything about music. There are only 10 (omitting Revelation): Matthew 26:30, Mark 14:26, Acts 16:25, Romans 15:9, 1 Corinthians 14:15, Ephesians 5:19, Colossians 3:16, Hebrews 2:12, Hebrews 13:15, and James 5:13. That's it! All refer exclusively to **vocal** music!

Here is the essential difference between those who support the instrument and those who do not. Those who oppose the instrument, say, "God told me to sing, so that's what I'm going to do." Those who support the instrument say, "God told me to sing, but I'm going to use an instrument, too."

Rick continues: "We all know thousands and thousands of sincere members of churches of Christ who have studied their Bible, and they no longer believe instrumental praise offends God." Once again, this is preposterous. Millions have come out of denominations and embraced the anti-instrument position. The World War 2 generation was composed almost entirely of such individuals. Rick's wild exaggeration is an insult to those who have done so—not to mention the millions upon millions of individuals who rejected instrumental music during the early centuries of Christianity and continued to do so even after the Catholic Church introduced it. The leaders of the Protestant Reformation movement were staunch opponents of instrumental music.

Further, Rick completely ignores the fact that multiplied millions of people embrace beliefs that even he would reject: 1.3 billion Muslims deny the deity of Christ; one billion atheists deny God exists; one billion Hindus believe in many gods; and the list goes on and on. Truth is not determined by sincerity or numbers. Rick is the victim of a very narrow, myopic perspective. He has surrounded himself for a number of years with the most liberal element among churches of Christ, and has come to assume that his acquaintances are representative of the larger mass of Christians scattered all over America and the world. The statistical evidence suggests that, while many numerically large churches of Christ have drifted to the left in the last 30 years, the rank and file membership of churches of Christ scattered across the nation have not fallen for the apostasy to which Rick has succumbed.

Rick claims personally to know hundreds of preachers "who love the Word of God, who can no longer teach the anti-instrument position, because they love the Bible too much to do it." Question: Surely Rick is aware of thousands of Methodist, Lutheran, and Presbyterian preachers who substitute sprinkling for immersion as baptism. Does Rick accuse them of lacking love for the Word of God? The audacity and arrogance of this attitude is seen in his remark: "Most of our pulpits of significance don't teach it." Unbelievable—and shameful. Talk about an inflated sense of importance (Proverbs 11:2; 13:10). "Pulpits of significance"? Which would those be and how are they determined? Is he referring to the preacher who stands behind the pulpit, or the size of the congregation? Is "significance" defined by mere **numbers**? Either way, Jesus certainly did not agree (Matthew 7:13-14; 1 Corinthians 1:26; Exodus 23:2; et al.). Rick claims: "I cannot in good conscience allow people to teach as Bible what the Bible doesn't teach." Yet, he admitted at the beginning of the sermon that he did precisely that **for 12 years**. He violated his conscience for over a decade—contrary to the will of God (Romans 14:23).

"What It Says About God"

Rick's second problem with the anti-instrument position is what he believes it says about God. He insists that God would not vacillate by liking one form of praise in one dispensation and disliking it in another. But I have already shown that it is not a matter of what God "likes." God required different worship practices at different times in history—everything from sacrificing animals, to offering drink and cereal offerings, to constructing a tabernacle, to burning incense, to sprinkling blood on a covenant box. God required Moses to **strike** the rock on one occasion, but only **speak** to the rock on another occasion. Even Rick is not prepared to say that since God "liked" these various forms of worship in one dispensation, He "likes" them now.

Who God Is

Rick continues:

> I do not believe that God so segregates life that what is acceptable in a car or at a wedding is not acceptable in a worship service. I do not believe God is gonna hand you a harp after He has sent millions to hell for mistakenly playing one. And most of all, most of all, when I read in my Bible about a God that was so desperate to save me, the sacrifice of His own Son was worth it to Him, I cannot accept that my relationship to that God could be jeopardized because I didn't discern His inference or interpret His silence? A God that would love me so much He would die for me, would send me to hell because I didn't properly understand something He never spoke about? That's not the God of the Bible. That's not the God of the cross. I believe God is passionately committed to saving a lost world.

If what is acceptable in a car or at a wedding is acceptable in a worship service, then we can honk car horns and throw rice in the assembly. Based on Psalm 149:5-6, we can move beds and swords into the assembly—"Let the saints rejoice in this honor and sing for joy **on their beds**" with "a **double-edged sword in their hands**" (Psalm 149:5-6)? The fact is that God **does** "segregate life" and that things right in themselves can be wrong religiously. Washing hands and eating barbecue are acceptable at home, but including barbecue on the Lord's Table and washing one's hands as an act of worship in the assembly would be sinful (cf. Matthew 15:2).

Rick's declaration that the loving God of the Bible and the cross would not send people to hell for using instruments reflects a fundamental, all-encompassing misconception inherent in his whole approach. *He conceptualizes a different God than the God of the Bible.* This attitude was apparent at the beginning of the sermon in the following words: "For over several decades, this church has heard a gospel of grace.... [W]e're simply now living out the implications of the gospel that we've been preaching here for a long, long time.... I believe churches of Christ across this country are ready for a revival of grace." "Grace" is redefined to mean "less restrictive," whereas grace in the New Testament is the compassion of God in sending His Son to die for us "while we were yet sinners" (Romans 5:8). In addition to misapprehending the biblical doctrine of grace (cf. Miller, 1996, pp. 307-313), Rick's view of God conflicts with the biblical record. We simply must return to a sincere study of the Word of God in order to make certain we have not fallen for a false portrait of God (see Chesser, 2004).

God is immutable, i.e., He does not change. He **always** has been a God of grace—even during the Patriarchal and Mosaic periods of human history. The very God that Rick insists would **never** condemn anyone for such a trivial, incidental thing as playing an instrument in praise to Him, nevertheless, is the God Who threatened to cut off individuals who used in private life the same blend of incense that was prepared for sacred purposes (Exodus 30:37-38). This is the same God of the Bible Who expelled the first human pair from Paradise for eating from one piece of fruit from one tree (Genesis 3). Nadab and Abihu were burned to death by God for incorporating foreign fire into their incense offering (Leviticus 10:1-2). God excluded Moses from entrance into the Promised Land because of one mistake at Kadesh—striking a rock instead of speaking to it (Numbers 20:7-12). God rejected Saul as king over Israel for altering His instructions only slightly (1 Samuel 15). God struck Uzzah dead for merely reaching out and steadying the Ark of the Covenant (2 Samuel 6:6-7). God rejected Uzziah because he entered the temple without authority merely to burn incense in worship (2 Chronicles 26). This is the same God Who threatened to **wipe out the entire nation of Israel** on five separate occasions due to their disobedience (Exodus 32:10; Numbers 14:12; 16:21,45; 25:11). Was He the God of grace on those occasions? If Rick desires to base his **worship** practice on the Old Testament, will he also accept the Old Testament's portrayal of God as One Who will **punish** people for altering His worship directives? Even in the New Testament, God executed two members of the church simply for misrepresenting the amount of money derived from the sale of their land (Acts 5), and He struck a man blind merely for attempting to dissuade a Roman proconsul from hearing Paul's preaching (Acts 13:11). Rick's characterization of God and grace contradict the Bible.

These instances could be multiplied many times over. They provide people with a healthy balance in their desperate need to know the God of the Bible. By redefining grace, Rick places himself among those who have fashioned God in their own image. Though one may pay lip service to the God of the Bible, one can so recast one's perception of God that He is no longer the God described on the pages of the Bible. The same may be said for the current mischaracterizations of Jesus. Many have recast and refashioned the Jesus of the Bible into a different Being—one who is unconcerned about obedience and whose "grace" forgives everybody unconditionally. They are worshipping a different Jesus than the one depicted in the New Testament. They have so misrepresented the person, nature, and conduct of Jesus that, for all practical purposes, they are giving allegiance to a concocted Jesus that does not exist—even as the Quran's depiction of God is skewed. The Quran has God saying and doing things that the God of the Bible simply would not say or do (Miller, 2005, pp. 169ff.). Likewise, those who misrepresent the Bible doctrine of grace have sufficiently **redefined** Jesus and God as to show they have a distorted grasp of deity.

The Jesus of the New Testament issued stern warnings about proper worship: "God is Spirit, and those who worship Him **must** worship in spirit and truth" (John 4:24, emp. added). "These people draw near to Me with their mouth, and honor Me with their lips, but their heart is far from Me. And **in vain they worship Me**, teaching as doctrines **the commandments of men**" (Matthew 15:8-9, emp. added). Instrumental music in Christian worship is a command of men. Imagine the fury and disgust that God must have for those who boldly encourage people to worship Him by using instruments without His permission. The Greek term for "hell" (*gehenna*) is used 12 times in the Greek New Testament—with 11 of those occurrences coming from Jesus' own mouth. Is that the Jesus of "grace" that Rick claims to represent in his preaching? Frank Chesser well-summarized the malady that grips Richland Hills and so many other churches that have drifted to the left in the last three decades:

> Liberalism preaches a grace that it does not understand and to which it will not listen. Grace furnishes a pattern for entrance into God's presence, but liberalism denies even the concept of a pattern. Grace teaches, but liberalism will not learn. Grace tugs at man's heart, imploring him to move in harmony with its melody, but liberalism is too busy marching to the beat of its own drum. If liberalism were teachable it would cease to exist (2001, p. 36).

Credibility Gap?

Rick then explained:

> But here's our problem: We are creating a serious credibility gap, because we don't even attempt any longer to defend from the Bible what we practice. If someone out in that atrium asks me, "I saw that you baptized someone today, why did you do that?" I open my Bible and show them. "And I saw that you shared

what you call communion together, why do you do that?" I open my Bible and I show them. "And I saw that you only sing *a cappella*, why do you do that?" I don't open my Bible.

How sad. All he would need to do is to open his Bible to Ephesians 5:19, Colossians 3:16, and other verses that would show the inquirer where God told Christians to sing. That is precisely why we sing. To see the fallacy in Rick's reasoning, a more fitting scenario would have been for a person in the atrium to ask, "Why don't you play instruments?" In that case Rick's response ("I don't open my Bible") would have been entirely appropriate, since he cannot open his New Testament and show where instruments are authorized. He could have then politely explained to the inquirer that we worship in harmony with God's directives and do not presume to add to His instructions (1 Corinthians 4:6; 2 John 9). He could have gently explained, "We strive to conform ourselves to the Bible; if you will show us a passage in the New Testament that instructs us to play an instrument to God, we certainly will comply." If Rick really thinks that no one defends New Testament worship anymore, he obviously has isolated himself from a sizable segment of the brotherhood. **Many** are those who continue to teach, preach, practice—**and defend from the Bible**—New Testament worship protocol.

When Rick insists, "I believe God is passionately committed to saving a lost world," he leaves the impression that God's passion to save people will not permit Him to be "nit-picky" over whether a person uses an instrument. Again, he has misapprehended who God is. Is God passionate about saving lost humanity? Absolutely! He wants all people to be saved, and made the ultimate sacrifice to make that possible (John 3:16; 1 Timothy 2:3-6; 2 Peter 3:9; 1 John 2:2). But the biblical facts of the matter are that the vast majority of the human race throughout world history will spend eternity in hell (Matthew 7:13-14; Luke 13:23-24). Why? Because they refuse to obey His will (Romans 6:16; 2 Corinthians 5:10; 2 Thessalonians 1:8; Hebrews 5:9; 2 John 6). That's no reflection on God's desire that every soul be saved; it is a reflection of the refusal of most people to set aside personal preference in order to please God. Rick has pitted the passion that God has for saving people against God's insistence that people love Him enough to obey Him.

Summary

We are living in a culture that pays lip service to religion, while fashioning that religion in accordance with human desire. Perhaps more than ever before in American culture, the focus is on assuaging fleshly desires and elevating human personalities, as Paul predicted: "For the time will come when men will not put up with sound doctrine. Instead, to suit their own desires, they will gather around them a great number of teachers to say what their itching ears want to hear. They will turn their ears away from the truth and turn aside to myths" (2 Timothy 4:3-4, NIV). Is it any wonder that Rick's second sermon received a standing ovation?

"THE BOTH/AND CHURCH—PART 3"

In this sermon, Rick addressed the question of whether it is biblically permissible to meet on Saturday instead of Sunday, and whether partaking of the Lord's Supper on Saturday is scriptural.

Sabbath for Man

Rick claims that the day does not matter since "the Sabbath is made for man, not the other way around." This claim, too, is a misunderstanding of the principle Jesus articulated (see Miller, 1996, pp. 410ff.). Rick implies the expression means that since God made the Sabbath for man, if human need necessitates it, one can occasionally violate Sabbath requirements—a false concept if there ever was one (e.g., Numbers 15:32-36). In reality, the meaning of Jesus' statement in Mark 2:27 is that God built into the Sabbath law a compassionate regard for both man and animal—and no one should violate the very precepts that God designed for man's good. However, the Jews of Jesus' day had corrupted God's original intentions by placing their own **added** restrictions and misinterpretations on the people, thereby losing sight of the original Sabbath laws (see Miller, 1996, pp. 410ff.; Miller, 2003b). Further, the fact that every day belongs to God does not nullify the fact that God can and has set aside certain days and required people to observe those days in special ways (e.g., the Sabbath). When Rick insists that such matters as the specific day of worship never were an issue in the early church, he ignores the fact that neither was voodoo, Islam, or Buddhism. But that does not prove that such matters were indifferent to God. Once again, Rick stakes his case on silence, rather than on the clear pronouncements of Scripture that allude to Sunday assembly.

Romans 14:5

Rick appeals to Romans 14:5 in order to insist that each member of the church has the right to choose on what day he or she will worship God and partake of the Lord's Supper—whether Saturday or Sunday. Yet the "days" of Romans 14:5 have nothing to do with whether God has designated Sunday as the day on which the church is to come together in the corporate worship assembly. The context pertains to the **non**religious selection of foods and **non**religious observance of days. The chapter discusses actions that are indifferent **to God**, allowing each person to exercise his or her own preference. Where God has spoken decisively, as He did in the case of Sunday worship (e.g., Acts 20:7; 1 Corinthians 16:2; Revelation 1:10), one must conform to God's will.

How will Rick harmonize his views with Galatians 4:10-11?—"You observe days and months and seasons and years. I am afraid for you, lest I have labored for you in vain." Romans 14:5 indicates observance of days is a matter of indifference, while Galatians 4:10-11 condemns the special observance of days. How do we harmonize these surface differences? Romans 14 concerns the **non**religious observance of a day (like a birthday or national holiday, e.g., July 4th), while Galatians 4 is about the **unauthorized religious** observance of days. Washing one's hands is not wrong in and of itself, since it is simply part of the overall care of the body that is authorized by God. However, incorporating the washing of hands into **religious** activity is condemned by Jesus (Mark 7:5-8). So it is with instruments.

Communion on Saturday

After giving assurance that Richland Hills "remains fully committed to the observance of weekly communion," Rick turned his attention to whether the Bible permits Saturday observance of the Lord's Supper. He claims that the first-century church partook of the Lord's Supper daily. He claims that "break bread" always refers to the Lord's Supper. He claims that the way first-century Christians reckoned time justifies observing the Lord's Supper on Saturday. Referring to Acts 20:7, Rick asks: "Let me say again, folks, let's remember the place of examples. Does what one church did at one time settle what all churches have to do at all times?" He claims that "in Troas, they used Roman time," and that Luke was a Gentile, and therefore the chronology of Acts 20:7 does not fit Jewish time. Hence, they met on Sunday evening, and the observance of the Lord's Supper occurred on Monday morning. He concludes: "The pre-eminent text that we have used in churches of Christ for years to prove you can only have communion on Sunday is about a church that had communion on Monday." He then asks: "Can an example of a church override a command from the Lord?" He has misunderstood the nature of biblical "examples" (see Warren, 1975). Rather than lengthen this book unnecessarily, the reader is urged to read the material already published on this subject that demonstrates that the first-century church—under the guidance and endorsement of the inspired apostles—partook of the Lord's Supper **every** Sunday and **only** on Sunday (Lyons, 2005; Miller, 1996, pp. 267-273; Miller, 2003c).

He then claims that *hosakis* ("whenever" or "as often as") in 1 Corinthians 11:25-26 means that frequency does not matter. He cites Robertson's statement that "*hosakis* is only used with the notion of indefinite repetition" (1934, p. 973). But Rick has misunderstood Robertson. By "indefinite repetition," Robertson meant that repetition is inherent in the construction without specifying the precise pattern of frequency—even as the English renderings "whenever" and "as often as" are indefinite. He did **not** mean that specific frequency is inherently **excluded**. He simply meant you cannot determine what that frequency is from *hosakis* alone. One must look elsewhere to see if any specific frequency is expressed. All one need do is read forward five chapters to find that frequency. The Corinthians knew that they were to meet **every** first day of the week—as is evident from the use of *kata* in 1 Corinthians 16:2 ("**every** week"—NIV, NASB). So for Paul to say, "As often as you meet, you are to do such and so," he knew that specificity about the day (Sunday) already was understood by his audience as taught by him in previous correspondence (Acts 18:1,11; 1 Corinthians 5:9).

Why First-Century Omission?

After this brief attempt to justify Saturday communion, Rick returned to the matter of instrumental music by acknowledging that the first-century church (as well as the synagogue) worshipped *a cappella*—an admission he earlier denied. Not accepting that this exclusion was by divine design, he offered several possible reasons for this omission based on various extrabiblical circumstances, and then concluded: "Here's the point: in their culture, for the reasons we just mentioned, it was the culturally appropriate and it was the missionally strategic thing to do to reach their culture to worship the way they did." He claims that no "church father" condemned instrumental music until the third century. He cites Clement of Alexandria from the second century as an instance of approving instrumental praise—though he admits the allusion is to **social** settings (see the previous remarks regarding Rick's superficial and unsubstantiated assertions regarding the patristic evidence).

He then likens instrumental music to four-part harmony and church buildings—things that are strictly optional. He insists that it is culturally strategic in American culture to add instruments in the same way that we have utilized updated English translations, more informal clothing, and shorter worship periods. He insists that the Gospel must be packaged in a culturally relevant form—in the same way that Jesus became flesh. Since instrumental music is so culturally prominent, the Gospel must be packaged to include it so that a bridge may be built to the lost.

But instrumental music was prominent in first-century culture. Rick, himself, admitted as much when he cited one possible reason for the early church's exclusion of instruments from worship: instruments were so prominent in contemporaneous culture and were associated with **paganism**. Indeed, those first-century Christians recognized we must refrain from identifying ourselves with secularism—the very thing Rick is urging. Much music in American culture, particularly since the Sixties, has been associated with drugs, alcohol, divorce, sex, crime, etc. Why associate the Gospel with such cultural decadence?

He also claims: "You see, this generation, unlike previous generations, does not view music as **entertainment**." He claims that post-modern people do not trust the media for their information, and so rely on musicians and artists for their messages. Two reactions: (1) we **still** must do **only** what God says—regardless of how far people alienate themselves from the simple communication form selected by God Himself, i.e., preaching and teaching (1 Corinthians 1:21; 2 Timothy 4:1-4); (2) throughout world history, music has always had a message and been related to current culture; what culture does **not** have music as part of its peculiar cultural circumstances? But that does not mean that its message is completely detached from entertainment, self-stimulation, amusement, and pleasure.

Rick asks: "If our burden is to reach the lost, is our fellowship courageous enough to face the possibility, and I would say even the probability, that our exclusive music preference hinders our evangelistic efforts?" As noted earlier, this is a shallow, fleshly assessment of evangelism. It completely ignores the fact that the power to reach people and transform their lives lies—not in **instrumental music**—but in **the Gospel of Christ** (Romans 1:16). Instrumental music is a cheap, inferior, manmade substitute that merely distracts people from true spirituality.

Rick alluded to a study that concluded that the single, pre-eminent reason people leave churches of Christ involves **worship**. That is a telling finding that demonstrates—not that we should adjust our worship to suit people—but that people throughout Bible history have manifested dissatisfaction with the simple, unpretentious worship that God has always specified (e.g., Cain, Nadab/Abihu, Saul, Uzziah, et al.). Legion are those in Bible history who "left" God because they wanted to worship their way, rather than conform their practice to

God's way (cf. 1 Kings 18; 2 Chronicles 26:16ff.). Tragic? Certainly! But no justification for corrupting pure worship by introducing instrumental music. If that is what it takes to evangelize the world and "keep" our children (a ludicrous idea, at best), God would have us to refrain. The solution is **not** to bring Hollywood into the church by providing people with the smoke and mirrors and the bravado that current culture craves.

By Rick's standards, Noah failed miserably to adapt to culture, repackage God's message, and bring in the big numbers—since only seven others (his own family) responded positively to his evangelistic efforts that lasted over a century. If Rick had been there, would he have chided Noah, urging him to change his mission strategy in order to be more relevant to the culture of his day? Would he make the same remarks to Noah that he made in his sermon: "I know this, if our fellowship stays on the course we are currently on, the future looks bleak. Someone has got to be a leader"? After all, by Rick's standards, Noah and his little group hardly qualified as a "pulpit of significance." By Rick's reasoning, if Noah had advocated enhancing worship with instrumental music and praise teams, he might have made some converts. But such "conversions" would not be legitimate in God's sight (Matthew 23:15). Though it is true that only eight people were saved at that point in history (1 Peter 3:20) and Noah failed to attract converts, the problem was neither the preacher (deemed by God "a preacher of righteousness" [2 Peter 2:5]), nor the packaging of the message; the problem was in **the hearts of the people**—their unwillingness to accept God's directives on His terms. So it is today.

CONCLUSION

If Rick had presented a genuinely biblical case proving the acceptability of instrumental music in worship, I would have been delighted to embrace the truth and commend Rick for his assistance. But the fact is that Rick offered no new "proofs" for instrumental music, and the "proofs" that he offered have long ago been weighed in the balances and found wanting (Daniel 5:27). Neither his three Old Testament reasons nor his five New Testament reasons justify instrumental music. Rick insisted that we are to be guided solely by the Bible and not by man's inferences and deductions. Yet he spent three sermons offering his own inferences and deductions—guilty of the very thing he attributes to "anti-instrumentalists."

The decision by Richland Hills to endorse instrumental music is simply another illicit change among others that have been made there in recent years. It was not always so. In the Articles of Incorporation for the Richland Hills Church of Christ, filed in the Office of the Secretary of State of Texas on November 2, 1967, Article Four, Section (e) reads: "That no mechanical musical instrument of any kind whatsoever shall ever be used in connection with the song service or worship or work to be carried on or conducted by said congregation or religious body" ("Articles of Incorporation...," p. 2). Article Five states that while the Elders shall be selected by the members of the congregation,

> no person shall be eligible to participate in any such selection of Elders who does not subscribe in and to the provisions and conditions of the teachings of the New Testament, **as enumerated in ARTICLE FOUR** hereof, and no person shall be eligible **to act as an Elder** within the corporation **unless** he be a loyal member of said congregation and in good standing and fully subscribing to the teachings of the New Testament **as enumerated in ARTICLE FOUR** hereof (p. 2, emp. added, capitals in orig.).

Article Five also states:

> In the event any Elder of the corporation at any time shall fail to subscribe to the teachings of the New Testament, as set forth in ARTICLE FOUR hereof, then upon such a determination by a majority of the Elders of the corporation, **he shall automatically become disqualified and dropped**

as an Elder of the corporation (p. 2, emp. added, capitals in orig.).

Observe that the organizers of the Richland Hills Church of Christ fully anticipated precisely what now has happened. They even placed legal (not to mention moral and scriptural) safeguards to insure that the congregation never introduced instrumental music. These legal stipulations prohibited any person becoming an elder if he endorsed instrumental music. No member could install an elder who endorsed instrumental music. And should a man be appointed an elder who did not believe in instrumental music, but who, in the course of time, changed his mind on the matter, he was to be removed ("dropped") from the eldership. This fool proof arrangement logically meant that all persons who desired to introduce instrumental music into their worship would have to **leave Richland Hills** and start their own church to do so. They could not **legally or morally** introduce it at Richland Hills.

Somewhere along the way **the law was broken**. Those who installed the first elder who endorsed instrumental music violated the law by participating in the selection process, and the elder who allowed himself to be installed violated the law for failing to subscribe to the Articles of Incorporation. His fellow elders violated the law by failing to dismiss him from the eldership. Whatever Rick may say about the propriety of introducing instrumental music—even if the Bible sanctions it—those who paved the way for it to happen at Richland Hills were **lawbreakers who lacked moral integrity in meeting their legal obligations.**

On February 1, 1994, the Richland Hills Articles of Incorporation were "amended and restated" ("Amended and Restated..."). They were adopted "by the unanimous consent of the Board of Directors at a meeting held on the 15th day of December, 1993" as well as by "at least two-thirds" of a quorum of the membership on January 2, 1994 (p. 2). Article Four was reduced to a single sentence—thereby omitting all the doctrinal concerns previously listed (p. 2). Article Five was completely rewritten to eliminate the safeguards regarding elder selection qualifications (pp. 2-4). Nevertheless, Article Five, Section 6 defined "Church of Christ" as, among other things, a body of believers who "assemble on **the first day of every week** to honor God and spiritually edify each other by observing the Lord's Supper; by studying the Bible, by contributing; by praying to God, and by singing songs of praise and edification **without the use of mechanical instruments**" (p. 4). At this point in the history of Richland Hills—1994—a majority of both the members and the elders still believed that the Lord's Supper was to be taken **every Sunday**, and that singing was to **exclude** instrumental music. It is interesting that 1994 was the same year that Rick claims the Holy Spirit chided him for not speaking out in support of instrumental music.

A third change was made to the Articles of Incorporation when "Articles of Amendment" were passed on November 15, 2006 and filed with the Office of the Secretary of State of Texas the next day—**exactly 17 days before Rick preached the first sermon** on "The Both/And Church" ("Articles of Amendment..."). Only one amendment was altered: "Article 5, Section 6 of the Articles of Incorporation was deleted in its entirety and replaced by the following" (p. 1). In the section that follows, two changes were made: "to assemble on the first day of every week..." was changed to "and who assemble every week..."—eliminating "first day"; and the phrase "and by singing songs of praise and edification without the use of mechanical instruments" was changed to "and singing songs of praise and edification" (p. 1). The way was now cleared for the introduction of instruments and Saturday observance of the Lord's Supper.

Over a century ago, many churches of Christ were swept into what was then called "the digression." The use of musical instruments in worship was one of the divisive issues that caused the breach. History is now repeating itself. The great tragedy of our own period of American history, for both the nation and the church, will surely be shown in the light of eternity to be the stampede to the left, the encroachment of secularism, the dulling of spiritual appetites in exchange for enshrining fleshly allurements, the shift from the rational to the emotional, in short—the betrayal of God. "Father forgive them, for they know not what they do."

REFERENCES

Abbott, T.K. (1897), *A Critical and Exegetical Commentary on the Epistles to the Ephesians and to the Colossians* (Edinburgh: T. & T. Clark).

Alexander, Joseph A. (1873), *The Psalms Translated and Explained* (Grand Rapid, MI: Baker, 1975 reprint).

Alford, Henry (1856), *Alford's Greek Testament* (Grand Rapids, MI: Baker, 1980 reprint).

Allen, Leslie (1997), *"zamar,"* New International Dictionary of Old Testament Theology and Exegesis, ed. Willem VanGemeren (Grand Rapids, MI: Zondervan).

"Amended and Restated Articles of Incorporation of Richland Hills Church of Christ, Fort Worth, Texas" (1994), [On-line], URL: https://direct.sos.state.tx.us.

American Heritage Dictionary of the English Language (2000), (Boston, MA: Houghton Mifflin), fourth edition.

Arndt, William F. and F. Wilbur Gingrich (1957), *A Greek-English Lexicon of the New Testament* (Chicago, IL: The University of Chicago Press).

"Articles of Amendment to Articles of Incorporation of Richland Hills Church of Christ" (2006), [On-line], URL: https://direct.sos.state.tx.us.

"Articles of Incorporation of Richland Hills Church of Christ, Fort Worth, Texas" (1967), [On-line], URL: https://direct.sos.state.tx.us.

Atchley, Rick (2006), "The Both/And Church—Parts 1-3," Richland Hills Church of Christ, December 3,10,17, [On-line], URL: http://www.rhcc.us/audio.php?pagecount=3&a=1&b=2.

Bales, James (1973), *Instrumental Music and New Testament Worship* (Searcy, AR: James D. Bales).

Balz, Horst and Gerhard Schneider (1993), *Exegetical Dictionary of the New Testament* (Grand Rapids, MI: Eerdmans).

Barnes, Albert (1847a), *Notes on the Old Testament: Psalms* (Grand Rapids, MI: Baker, 2005 reprint).

Barnes, Albert (1847b), *Notes on the Old Testament: Ephesians* (Grand Rapids, MI: Baker, 2005 reprint).

Bartels, K.H. (1978), *"psalmos," The New International Dictionary of New Testament Theology*, ed. Colin Brown (Grand Rapids, MI: Zondervan, sixth printing).

Barth, Karl (1980), *"zamar, zamir, zimrah, mizmor," Theological Dictionary of the Old Testament*, ed. G. Johannes Botterweck and Helmer Ringgren (Grand Rapids, MI: Eerdmans).

Berry, George R. (1897a), *Greek-English Lexicon to the New Testament* (Grand Rapids, MI: Zondervan, 1958 reprint).

Berry, George R. (1897b), *The Interlinear Greek-English New Testament* (Grand Rapids, MI: Zondervan, 1958 reprint).

Betz, Otto (1976), *"exousia," The New International Dictionary of New Testament Theology*, ed. Colin Brown (Grand Rapids, MI: Zondervan).

Biblia Hebraica Stuttgartensia (1967/77), (Stuttgart: Deutsche Bibelstiftung).

Bietenhard, Hans (1976), *"onoma," The New International Dictionary of New Testament Theology*, ed. Colin Brown (Grand Rapids, MI: Zondervan).

Blass, F. and A. Debrunner (1961), *A Greek Grammar of the New Testament*, trans. Robert Funk (Chicago, IL: The University of Chicago Press).

Brown, Francis, S.R. Driver, and Charles B. Briggs (1906), *A Hebrew and English Lexicon of the Old Testament* (Peabody, MA: Hendrickson), eighth printing.

Bruce, F.F. (1984), *The Epistles to the Colossians, to Philemon, and to the Ephesians* (Grand Rapids, MI: Eerdmans).

Bullinger, E.W. (1898), *Figures of Speech Used in the Bible* (Grand Rapids, MI: Baker, 1968 reprint).

Calvin, John (1999 reprint), *Commentary on the Book of Psalms*, trans. James Anderson (Grand Rapids, MI: Baker).

Chamberlain, William D. (1941), *An Exegetical Grammar of the Greek New Testament* (Grand Rapids, MI: Baker).

Chesser, Frank (2001), *The Spirit of Liberalism* (Huntsville, AL: Publishing Designs).

Chesser, Frank (2004), *Portrait of God* (Huntsville, AL: Publishing Designs).

Clarke, Adam (no date), *A Commentary and Critical Notes: Job-Solomon's Song* (Nashville, TN: Abingdon-Cokesbury).

Conybeare, W.J. and J.S. Howson (1899), *The Life and Epistles of Saint Paul* (Hartford, CT: S.S. Scranton).

Dana, H.E. and Julius Mantey (1927), *A Manual Grammar of the Greek New Testament* (Toronto, Ontario: Macmillan).

Danker, Frederick W. (2000), *A Greek-English Lexicon of the New Testament and Other Early Christian Literature* (Chicago, IL: University of Chicago Press), third edition.

Davidson, Benjamin (1848), *The Analytical Hebrew and Chaldee Lexicon* (Grand Rapids, MI: Zondervan), 1970 reprint.

Deaver, Roy (1987), *Ascertaining Bible Authority* (Austin, TX: Firm Foundation Publishing House).

Delling, Gerhard (1972), "*humnos, humneo, psallo, psalmos,*" *Theological Dictionary of the New Testament*, ed. Gerhard Friedrich (Grand Rapids, MI: Eerdmans).

DeWelt, Don (1985), "Letter to the Editor," *Gospel Advocate*, 127[10]:293, May 16.

Dungan, D.R. (1888), *Hermeneutics* (Delight, AR: Gospel Light).

Eadie, John (1883), *A Commentary on the Greek Text of the Epistle of Paul to the Ephesians* (Grand Rapids, MI: Baker, 1979 reprint).

Eadie, John (1884), *A Commentary on the Greek Text of the Epistle of Paul to the Colossians* (Grand Rapids, MI: Baker, 1979 reprint).

Edersheim, Alfred (1874), *The Temple: Its Ministry and Services* (Grand Rapids, MI: Eerdmans, 1972 reprint).

Edersheim, Alfred (1915), *The Life and Times of Jesus the Messiah* (New York: Longmans, Green, & Co.), eighth edition.

Edwards, R.B. (1988 reprint), "Woman," *The International Standard Bible Encyclopedia*, ed. Geoffrey Bromiley (Grand Rapids, MI: Eerdmans).

Fee, Gordon and Douglas Stuart (1982), *How to Read the Bible For All its Worth* (Grand Rapids, MI: Zondervan).

Ferguson, Everett (1971), *Early Christians Speak* (Austin, TX: Sweet Publishing).

Ferguson, Everett (1972), *A Cappella Music in the Public Worship of the Church* (Abilene, TX: ACU Press), 1999 edition.

Ferguson, Everett (1987), "Early Church History and the Instrumental Music Controversy," in *The Instrumental Music Issue*, ed. Bill Flatt (Nashville, TN: Gospel Advocate).

Gesenius, William (1847), *Hebrew and Chaldee Lexicon to the Old Testament* (Grand Rapids, MI: Baker, 1979 reprint).

Gietmann, G. (1910), "Ecclesiastical Music," *The Catholic Encyclopedia* (New York: Robert Appleton), [On-line], URL: http://www.newadvent.org/cathen/10648a.htm.

Gingrich, F. Wilbur (1965), *Shorter Lexicon of the Greek New Testament* (Chicago, IL: The University of Chicago Press).

Girardeau, John (1888), *Instrumental Music in the Public Worship of the Church* (Wiggins, MS: Apologia Press, 2000 reprint).

Girdlestone, Robert B. (1983), *Synonyms of the Old Testament* (Grand Rapids, MI: Baker), third edition.

Graetz, Heinrich (1893), *The History of the Jews* (Philadelphia, PA: The Jewish Publication Society of America).

Hackett, H.B., ed. (1870), *Smith's Dictionary of the Bible* (New York: Hurd & Houghton).

Hanna, Robert (1983), *A Grammatical Aid to the Greek New Testament* (Grand Rapids, MI: Baker).

Harper, William R. and Revere F. Weidner (1888), *An Introductory New Testament Method* (New York: Charles Scribner's Sons).

Hickie, W.J. (1893), *Greek-English Lexicon to the New Testament* (Grand Rapids, MI: Baker, 1977 reprint).

Holladay, William (1971), *A Concise Hebrew and Aramaic Lexicon of the Old Testament* (Grand Rapids, MI: Eerdmans).

Jackson, Don (1979), "A Long Overdue Correction," *Gospel Advocate*, 121[10]:152-153, March 8.

Johnson, B.W. (1889), *The People's New Testament* (Delight, AR: Gospel Light Publishing).

Keil, C.F. and F. Delitzsch (1976a reprint), *Commentary on the Old Testament: Psalms* (Grand Rapids, MI: Eerdmans).

Keil, C.F. and F. Delitzsch (1976b reprint), *Commentary on the Old Testament: The Pentateuch* (Grand Rapids, MI: Eerdmans).

Kubo, Sakae (1975), *A Reader's Greek-English Lexicon of the New Testament* (Grand Rapids, MI: Zondervan).

Kuhner, Raphael (1853), *Grammar of the Greek Language*, trans. B.B. Edwards and S.H. Taylor (New York: D. Appleton).

Kurfees, M.C. (1911), *Instrumental Music in the Worship* (Nashville, TN: Gospel Advocate, 1975 reprint).

Leupold, H.C. (1959), *Exposition of the Psalms* (Grand Rapids, MI: Baker, 1969 reprint).

Lewis, Jack P. (1987), "New Testament Authority for Music in Worship," in *The Instrumental Music Issue*, ed. Bill Flatt (Nashville, TN: Gospel Advocate).

Liddell, Henry G. and Robert Scott (1843), *A Greek-English Lexicon* (Oxford, England: Clarendon), ninth edition.

Lightfoot, J.B. (1859), *A Commentary on the New Testament from the Talmud and Hebraica* (Grand Rapids, MI: Baker, 1979 reprint).

Lightfoot, J.B. (1875), *St. Paul's Epistles to the Colossians and to Philemon* (London: MacMillan).

Lincoln, Andrew (1990), *Word Biblical Commentary: Ephesians* (Dallas, TX: Thomas Nelson).

Lyons, Eric (2005), "'Breaking Bread' on the 'First Day' of the Week," [On-line], URL: http://www.apologeticspress.org/articles/343.

Machen, J. Gresham (1923), *New Testament Greek for Beginners* (Toronto, Ontario: Macmillan).

McClintock, John and James Strong (1867-1881), *Cyclopedia of Biblical, Theological, and Ecclesiastical Literature* (Grand Rapids, MI: Baker, 1969-1970 reprint).

McCord, Hugo (1962), "Arndt-Gingrich to be Corrected," *Gospel Advocate*, 104[44]:688,695, November 1.

McCord, Hugo (1964), "A Disappointment," *Gospel Advocate*, 106[34]:539-540, August 20.

McCord, Hugo (1990), "The Psallo Argument," *Spiritual Sword*, 21[4]:27-30, July.

McGarvey, J.W. (1892), *New Commentary on Acts of Apostles* (Cincinnati, OH: Standard).

McGarvey, J.W. (1910), *Biblical Criticism* (Cincinnati, OH: Standard Publishing).

McGarvey, J.W. (no date), *The Fourfold Gospel* (Cincinnati, OH: Standard).

McKinnon, James (1965), *The Church Fathers and Musical Instruments* (Ann Arbor, MI: University Microfilms).

Mickelsen, A. Berkeley (1963), *Interpreting the Bible* (Grand Rapids, MI: Eerdmans, 1987 reprint).

Miller, Dave (1996), *Piloting the Strait* (Pulaski, TN: Sain Publishing).

Miller, Dave (2003a), "Modern-Day Miracles, Tongue-Speaking, and Holy Spirit Baptism: A Refutation—EXTENDED VERSION," *Reason & Revelation,* 23[3]:17-23, [On-line], URL: http://www.apologeticspress.org/articles/2569.

Miller, Dave (2003b), "Situationism," [On-line], URL: http://www.apologeticspress.org/articles/2266.

Miller, Dave (2003c), "Sunday and the Lord's Supper," [On-line], URL: http://www.apologeticspress.org/articles/2304.

Miller, Dave (2005), *The Quran Unveiled* (Montgomery, AL: Apologetics Press).

Moulton, James H. and George Milligan (1930), *The Vocabulary of the Greek Testament* (Grand Rapids, MI: Eerdmans, 1982 reprint).

Nicoll, W. Robertson (no date), *The Expositor's Greek Testament* (Grand Rapids, MI: Eerdmans).

Otten, Joseph (1911), "Musical Instruments in Church Services," *The Catholic Encyclopedia* (New York: Robert Appleton), [On-line], URL: http://www.newadvent.org/cathen/10657a.htm.

Peloubet, F.N. (1947), *Peloubet's Bible Dictionary* (Philadelphia, PA: John C. Winston Company).

Perschbacher, Wesley, ed. (1990), *The New Analytical Greek Lexicon* (Peabody, MA: Hendrickson).

Robertson, A.T. (1931), *Word Pictures in the New Testament: The Epistles of Paul* (Nashville, TN: Broadman).

Robertson, A.T. (1934), *A Grammar of the Greek New Testament in the Light of Historical Research* (Nashville, TN: Broadman).

Robinson, Edward (1879), *Greek and English Lexicon of the New Testament* (New York: Harper & Brothers).

Robinson, Edward (1881), *The Comprehensive Critical and Explanatory Bible Encyclopedia* (Toledo, OH: H.W. Snow).

Ross, Bobby (2007), "Nation's Largest Church of Christ Adding Instrumental Service," *Christian Chronicle*, December 12, [Online], URL: http://www.christianchronicle.org/modules.php?name=News&file=article&sid=555&mode=&order=0&thold=0.

Salmond, S.D.F. (no date), *The Expositor's Greek Testament: The Epistle to the Ephesians*, ed. W. Robertson Nicoll (Grand Rapids, MI: Eerdmans).

Schlier, Heinrich (1964), *"ado, ode," Theological Dictionary of the New Testament*, ed. Gerhard Kittel (Grand Rapids, MI: Eerdmans).

Schurer, Emil (1890), *A History of the Jewish People in the Time of Jesus Christ* (Grand Rapids, MI: Hendrickson, 1995 reprint).

The Septuagint Version (1970 reprint), (Grand Rapids, MI: Zondervan).

Smith, G. Abbott (1937), *A Manual Greek Lexicon of the New Testament* (New York: Charles Scribner's Sons).

Spence, H.D.M. and J.S. Exell, eds. (1958 reprint), "Colossians," *The Pulpit Commentary* (Grand Rapids, MI: Eerdmans).

Spence, H.D.M. and J.S. Exell, eds. (1961 reprint), "St. Matthew," *The Pulpit Commentary* (Grand Rapids, MI: Eerdmans).

Stark, J. Carroll and Joe S. Warlick (1903), *Stark-Warlick Debate* (Nashville, TN: McQuiddy Printing).

Stern, David, trans. (1995 reprint), *Jewish New Testament* (Clarksville, MD: Jewish New Testament Publications).

Summers, Ray (1950), *Essentials of New Testament Greek* (Nashville, TN: Broadman Press).

Thayer, Joseph H. (1901), *A Greek-English Lexicon of the New Testament* (Grand Rapids, MI: Baker, 1977 reprint).

VanGemeren, Willem (1991), *The Expositor's Bible Commentary: Psalms*, ed. Frank Gaebelein (Grand Rapids, MI: Zondervan).

VanGemeren, Willem, ed. (1997), *New International Dictionary of Old Testament Theology and Exegesis* (Grand Rapids, MI: Zondervan).

Vaughan, Curtis (1967), *The New Testament from 26 Translations* (Grand Rapids, MI: Zondervan).

Vincent, Marvin (1890), *Words Studies in the New Testament* (Grand Rapids, MI: Eerdmans, 1946 reprint).

Vine, W.E. (1940), *An Expository Dictionary of New Testament Words* (Old Tappan, NJ: Revell).

Wallace, Daniel B. (1996), *Greek Grammar: Beyond the Basics* (Grand Rapids, MI: Zondervan).

Warren, Thomas B. (1975), *When Is An "Example" Binding?* (Jonesboro, AR: National Christian Press).

Warren, Thomas B. (1982), *Logic and the Bible* (Jonesboro, AR: National Christian Press).

Warren, Thomas B. (1986), *The Bible Only makes Christians Only and the Only Christians* (Jonesboro, AR: National Christian Press).

Weakland, R.G. (1967), "History of Sacred Music," *The New Catholic Encyclopedia* (Washington, D.C.: The Catholic University of America).

Westerholm, Stephen (1988 reprint), "Temple," *The International Standard Bible Encyclopedia*, ed. Geoffrey Bromiley (Grand Rapids, MI: Eerdmans).

Westcott, B.A. and F.J.A. Hort (1964 reprint), *The New Testament in the Original Greek* (New York: MacMillan).

Wigram, George (1890), *The Englishman's Hebrew and Chaldee Concordance of the Old Testament* (Grand Rapids, MI: Baker, 1980 reprint).

Wolf, Herbert (1980), *"zamar," Theological Wordbook of the Old Testament*, ed. R. Laird Harris, Gleason Archer, Jr., and Bruce Waltke (Chicago, IL: Moody).

Wood, A. Skevington (1981), *The Expositor's Bible Commentary: Ephesians*, ed. Frank Gaebelein (Grand Rapids, MI: Zondervan).

Appendix A

Old Testament Occurrences of *zamar* in the Piel

The Translation of *zamar* in the Piel in English Versions

Verse/Version	sing	sing praise(s)	praise	give/chant praise	sing psalm(s)	make music	make melody	sing my hymn	praise in psalms	play
Judges 5:3										
KJV		✓								
NKJV		✓								
ASV		✓								
NASB		✓								
RSV							✓			
NIV						✓				
ESV							✓			
NEB					✓					
NAB (Catholic)								✓		
Harkavy (Jewish)		✓								
2 Samuel 22:50										
KJV		✓								
NKJV		✓								
ASV		✓								
NASB		✓								
RSV		✓								
NIV		✓								
ESV		✓								
NEB					✓					
NAB (Catholic)		✓								
Harkavy (Jewish)		✓								
1 Chronicles 16:9										
KJV					✓					
NKJV					✓					
ASV		✓								
NASB		✓								
RSV		✓								
NIV		✓								
ESV		✓								
NEB					✓					
NAB (Catholic)		✓								
Harkavy (Jewish)					✓					

The Translation of *zamar* in the Piel in English Versions

Verse/Version	sing	sing praise(s)	praise	give/chant praise	sing psalm(s)	make music	make melody	sing my hymn	praise in psalms	play
Psalm 7:17										
KJV		✓								
NKJV		✓								
ASV		✓								
NASB		✓								
RSV		✓								
NIV		✓								
ESV		✓								
NEB					✓					
NAB (Catholic)		✓								
Harkavy (Jewish)		✓								
Psalm 9:2										
KJV		✓								
NKJV		✓								
ASV		✓								
NASB		✓								
RSV		✓								
NIV		✓								
ESV		✓								
NEB									✓	
NAB (Catholic)		✓								
Harkavy (Jewish)		✓								
Psalm 9:11										
KJV		✓								
NKJV		✓								
ASV		✓								
NASB		✓								
RSV		✓								
NIV		✓								
ESV		✓								
NEB					✓					
NAB (Catholic)		✓								
Harkavy (Jewish)		✓								

The Translation of *zamar* in the Piel in English Versions

Verse/Version	sing	sing praise(s)	praise	give/chant praise	sing psalm(s)	make music	make melody	sing my hymn	praise in psalms	play
Psalm 18:49										
KJV		✓								
NKJV		✓								
ASV		✓								
NASB		✓								
RSV		✓								
NIV		✓								
ESV	✓									
NEB					✓					
NAB (Catholic)		✓								
Harkavy (Jewish)		✓								
Psalm 21:13										
KJV			✓							
NKJV			✓							
ASV			✓							
NASB			✓							
RSV			✓							
NIV			✓							
ESV			✓							
NEB					✓					
NAB (Catholic)				✓						
Harkavy (Jewish)			✓							
Psalm 27:6										
KJV		✓								
NKJV		✓								
ASV		✓								
NASB		✓								
RSV							✓			
NIV						✓				
ESV							✓			
NEB					✓					
NAB (Catholic)				✓						
Harkavy (Jewish)		✓								

The Translation of *zamar* in the Piel in English Versions

Verse/Version	sing	sing praise(s)	praise	give/chant praise	sing psalm(s)	make music	make melody	sing my hymn	praise in psalms	play
Psalm 30:4										
KJV	✓									
NKJV		✓								
ASV		✓								
NASB		✓								
RSV							✓			
NIV	✓									
ESV		✓								
NEB					✓					
NAB (Catholic)		✓								
Harkavy (Jewish)	✓									
Psalm 30:12										
KJV		✓								
NKJV		✓								
ASV		✓								
NASB		✓								
RSV					✓					
NIV		✓								
ESV		✓								
NEB		✓								
NAB (Catholic)		✓								
Harkavy (Jewish)		✓								
Psalm 33:2										
KJV	✓									
NKJV	✓									
ASV		✓								
NASB	✓									
RSV						✓				
NIV							✓			
ESV					✓					
NEB				✓						
NAB (Catholic)							✓			
Harkavy (Jewish)	✓									

The Translation of *zamar* in the Piel in English Versions

Verse/Version	sing	sing praise(s)	praise	give/chant praise	sing psalm(s)	make music	make melody	sing my hymn	praise in psalms	play
Psalm 47:6 (4 times)										
KJV		✓✓✓✓								
NKJV		✓✓✓✓								
ASV		✓✓✓✓								
NASB		✓✓✓✓								
RSV		✓✓✓✓								
NIV		✓✓✓✓								
ESV		✓✓✓✓								
NEB			✓✓						✓✓	
NAB (Catholic)		✓✓✓✓								
Harkavy (Jewish)		✓✓✓✓								
Psalm 47:7										
KJV		✓								
NKJV		✓								
ASV		✓+			✓+					
NASB		✓×			✓×					
RSV		✓*			✓*					
NIV		✓*			✓*					
ESV		✓			✓					
NEB					✓					
NAB (Catholic)		✓								
Harkavy (Jewish)		✓								
Psalm 57:7										
KJV				✓						
NKJV		✓								
ASV		✓								
NASB		✓								
RSV						✓				
NIV						✓	✓			
ESV							✓			
NEB								✓		
NAB (Catholic)				✓					✓*	
Harkavy (Jewish)				✓						

* NASB has "sing praises with a skillful psalm"
× RSV has "sing praises with a psalm"
× NIV has "sing to him a psalm of praise"
* NEB has "raise a psalm"

135

The Translation of *zamar* in the Piel in English Versions

Verse/Version	sing	sing praise(s)	praise	give/chant praise	sing psalm(s)	make music	make melody	sing my hymn	praise in psalms	play
Psalm 57:9										
KJV	✓									
NKJV	✓									
ASV		✓								
NASB		✓								
RSV	✓									
NIV		✓								
ESV		✓								
NEB									✓+	
NAB (Catholic)				✓						
Harkavy (Jewish)	✓									
Psalm 59:17										
KJV	✓									
NKJV		✓								
ASV		✓								
NASB		✓								
RSV		✓								
NIV		✓								
ESV		✓								
NEB									✓+	
NAB (Catholic)	✓	✓								
Harkavy (Jewish)		✓								
Psalm 61:8										
KJV		✓								
NKJV		✓								
ASV		✓								
NASB		✓								
RSV		✓								
NIV		✓								
ESV					✓					
NEB		✓								
NAB (Catholic)		✓								
Harkavy (Jewish)		✓								

+ NEB has "raise a psalm"

136

The Translation of *zamar* in the Piel in English Versions

Verse/Version	sing	sing praise(s)	praise	give/chant praise	sing psalm(s)	make music	make melody	sing my hymn	praise in psalms	play
Psalm 66:2										
KJV	✓									
NKJV	✓									
ASV	✓									
NASB	✓									
RSV	✓									
NIV	✓									
ESV	✓									
NEB									✓+	
NAB (Catholic)	✓	✓								
Harkavy (Jewish)	✓									
Psalm 66:4 (2 times)										
KJV	✓✓									
NKJV		✓✓								
ASV	✓✓									
NASB		✓✓								
RSV		✓✓								
NIV		✓✓								
ESV		✓✓								
NEB	✓				✓					
NAB (Catholic)		✓✓								
Harkavy (Jewish)	✓✓									
Psalm 68:4										
KJV		✓								
NKJV		✓								
ASV		✓								
NASB		✓								
RSV		✓								
NIV		✓								
ESV		✓								
NEB									✓×	
NAB (Catholic)				✓						
Harkavy (Jewish)		✓								

+ NEB has "let psalms declare"
× NEB has "raise a psalm"

137

The Translation of *zamar* in the Piel in English Versions

Verse/Version	sing	sing praise(s)	praise	give/chant praise	sing psalm(s)	make music	make melody	sing my hymn	praise in psalms	play
Psalm 68:32										
KJV		✓								
NKJV		✓								
ASV		✓								
NASB		✓								
RSV		✓								
NIV		✓								
ESV		✓								
NEB					✓					
NAB (Catholic)				✓						
Harkavy (Jewish)		✓								
Psalm 71:22										
KJV	✓									
NKJV	✓									
ASV		✓								
NASB		✓								
RSV		✓								
NIV		✓								
ESV		✓								
NEB		✓			✓					
NAB (Catholic)	✓									
Harkavy (Jewish)	✓									
Psalm 71:23										
KJV	✓									
NKJV		✓								
ASV		✓								
NASB		✓								
RSV		✓								
NIV		✓								
ESV										
NEB					✓					
NAB (Catholic)		✓								
Harkavy (Jewish)	✓									

The Translation of *zamar* in the Piel in English Versions

Verse/Version	sing	sing praise(s)	praise	give/chant praise	sing psalm(s)	make music	make melody	sing my hymn	praise in psalms	play
Psalm 75:9										
KJV		✓								
NKJV		✓								
ASV		✓								
NASB		✓								
RSV		✓								
NIV		✓								
ESV		✓								
NEB		✓								
NAB (Catholic)		✓								
Harkavy (Jewish)		✓								
Psalm 92:1										
KJV		✓								
NKJV		✓								
ASV		✓								
NASB		✓								
RSV		✓								
NIV						✓				
ESV		✓								
NEB					✓					
NAB (Catholic)		✓								
Harkavy (Jewish)		✓								
Psalm 98:4										
KJV		✓								
NKJV		✓								
ASV		✓								
NASB		✓								
RSV		✓								
NIV						✓+				
ESV		✓								
NEB					✓					
NAB (Catholic)		✓								
Harkavy (Jewish)		✓								

+ NIV has "with music"

139

The Translation of *zamar* in the Piel in English Versions

Verse/Version	sing	sing praise(s)	praise	give/chant praise	sing psalm(s)	make music	make melody	sing my hymn	praise in psalms	play
Psalm 98:5										
KJV	✓									
NKJV	✓									
ASV		✓								
NASB		✓								
RSV		✓								
NIV						✓				
ESV		✓								
NEB					✓					
NAB (Catholic)		✓								
Harkavy (Jewish)	✓									
Psalm 101:1										
KJV	✓									
NKJV		✓								
ASV		✓								
NASB		✓								
RSV	✓									
NIV		✓								
ESV						✓				
NEB									✓+	
NAB (Catholic)	✓									
Harkavy (Jewish)		✓								
Psalm 104:33										
KJV		✓								
NKJV		✓								
ASV		✓								
NASB		✓								
RSV		✓								
NIV		✓								
ESV		✓								
NEB					✓					
NAB (Catholic)		✓								
Harkavy (Jewish)		✓								

+ NEB has "raise a psalm"

The Translation of *zamar* in the Piel in English Versions

Verse/Version	sing	sing praise(s)	praise	give/chant praise	sing psalm(s)	make music	make melody	sing my hymn	praise in psalms	play
Psalm 105:2										
KJV					✓					
NKJV					✓					
ASV		✓								
NASB		✓								
RSV		✓								
NIV		✓								
ESV		✓								
NEB					✓+					
NAB (Catholic)										
Harkavy (Jewish)		✓								
Psalm 108:1										
KJV				✓						
NKJV				✓						
ASV		✓								
NASB		✓								
RSV							✓			
NIV						✓				
ESV							✓			
NEB									✓×	
NAB (Catholic)				✓						
Harkavy (Jewish)		✓								
Psalm 108:3										
KJV		✓								
NKJV		✓								
ASV		✓								
NASB		✓								
RSV		✓								
NIV	✓									
ESV		✓								
NEB									✓×	
NAB (Catholic)				✓						
Harkavy (Jewish)		✓								

+ NEB has "Pay him honour with song and psalm"

× NEB has "raise a psalm"

141

The Translation of *zamar* in the Piel in English Versions

Verse/Version	sing	sing praise(s)	praise	give/chant praise	sing psalm(s)	make music	make melody	sing my hymn	praise in psalms	play
Psalm 135:3										
KJV		✓								
NKJV		✓								
ASV		✓								
NASB		✓								
RSV	✓									
NIV		✓								
ESV	✓									
NEB									✓+	
NAB (Catholic)		✓								
Harkavy (Jewish)		✓								
Psalm 138:1										
KJV		✓								
NKJV		✓								
ASV		✓								
NASB		✓								
RSV		✓								
NIV		✓								
ESV		✓								
NEB					✓					
NAB (Catholic)		✓								
Harkavy (Jewish)		✓								
Psalm 144:9										
KJV		✓								
NKJV		✓								
ASV		✓								
NASB		✓								
RSV										✓
NIV						✓				
ESV										✓
NEB					✓×					
NAB (Catholic)				✓						
Harkavy (Jewish)	✓									

+ NEB has "honour his name with psalms"
× NEB has "psalms to the music of"

142

The Translation of *zamar* in the Piel in English Versions

Verse/Version	sing	sing praise(s)	praise	give/chant praise	sing psalm(s)	make music	make melody	sing my hymn	praise in psalms	play
Psalm 146:2										
KJV		✓								
NKJV		✓								
ASV		✓								
NASB		✓								
RSV		✓								
NIV		✓								
ESV					✓					
NEB										
NAB (Catholic)		✓								
Harkavy (Jewish)		✓								
Psalm 147:1										
KJV		✓								
NKJV		✓								
ASV		✓								
NASB		✓								
RSV		✓								
NIV		✓								
ESV		✓								
NEB					✓					
NAB (Catholic)		✓								
Harkavy (Jewish)		✓								
Psalm 147:7										
KJV		✓								
NKJV		✓								
ASV		✓								
NASB		✓								
RSV							✓			
NIV						✓				
ESV							✓			
NEB					✓					
NAB (Catholic)		✓								
Harkavy (Jewish)		✓								

The Translation of *zamar* in the Piel in English Versions

Verse/Version	sing	sing praise(s)	praise	give/chant praise	sing psalm(s)	make music	make melody	sing my hymn	praise in psalms	play
Psalm 149:3										
KJV		✓								
NKJV		✓								
ASV		✓								
NASB		✓								
RSV							✓			
NIV						✓				
ESV							✓			
NEB					✓					
NAB (Catholic)		✓								
Harkavy (Jewish)		✓								
Isaiah 12:5										
KJV	✓									
NKJV										
ASV	✓									
NASB		✓+								
RSV		✓								
NIV	✓									
ESV	✓									
NEB					✓					
NAB (Catholic)		✓								
Harkavy (Jewish)	✓									

+ NASB has "praise the Lord in song"

144

Appendix B

New Testament Occurrences of *psallo*

The Translation of *psallo* in English Versions

Verse/Version	sing	sing hymn(s)	sing praise(s)	sing psalm(s)	making melody	make music	chanting
Romans 15:9							
KJV	✓						
NKJV	✓						
ASV	✓						
NASB	✓						
RSV	✓						
NIV		✓					
ESV	✓						
NEB		✓					
TEV	✓		✓				
Jerusalem							
1 Corinthians 14:15 (2 times)							
KJV	✓✓						
NKJV	✓✓						
ASV	✓✓						
NASB	✓✓						
RSV	✓✓						
NIV	✓✓						
ESV	✓		✓				
NEB	✓	✓					
TEV	✓✓		✓✓				
Jerusalem							

The Translation of *psallo* in English Versions

Verse/Version	sing	sing hymn(s)	sing praise(s)	sing psalm(s)	making melody	make music	chanting
Ephesians 5:19							
KJV					✓		
NKJV					✓		
ASV					✓		
NASB					✓		
RSV					✓		
NIV						✓	
ESV					✓		
NEB						✓	
TEV			✓				
Jerusalem							✓
James 5:13							
KJV				✓			
NKJV				✓			
ASV			✓				
NASB			✓				
RSV			✓				
NIV			✓				
ESV			✓				
NEB			✓				
TEV				✓			
Jerusalem